National Defense Research Institute

T0096079

CUBA
CLEARING PERILOUS WATERS?

EDWARD GONZALEZ

Prepared for the
Office of the Secretary of Defense

RAND

Cuba's communist system is currently undergoing change. However, the outcome of that change is unclear. To determine whether the Cuban ship of state is heading toward perilous waters or smooth sailing, this report assesses the major civilian and military leaders and institutions in the Castro regime, the civil society groups emerging outside the regime, and the respective roles of all these actors in the years immediately ahead. It reviews current U.S. policy and evaluates how prevailing U.S. policy options may affect the internal balance of power among Cuban actors, and hasten or hinder the transition toward a democratic, market-oriented Cuba. It concludes by recommending a new, proactive policy for accelerating Cuba's transition. The Appendix describes four possible Cuban endgames that may materialize under current U.S. policy.

This report originated in the National Defense Research Institute's (NDRI's) project on "Actors, Outcomes, and U.S. Policy for a Cuba Undergoing Change," which was completed in September 1995. The NDRI client was the Office of the Assistant Secretary of Defense (International Security Affairs/Inter-American Affairs), in the Office of the Under Secretary of Defense for Policy. Revised and updated to include Cuban developments up to the beginning of December 1995 (with a Postscript including the February and March 1996 developments), the report supersedes an earlier draft submitted to the client in August 1995. The report builds on two previous RAND reports by the author and David Ronfeldt: *Cuba Adrift in a Postcommunist World*, R-4231-USDP, 1992, and *Storm Warnings for Cuba*, MR-452-OSD, 1994. The report addresses the needs of U.S. policymakers and analysts concerned with Cuba, but it also should be of interest to a wider audience.

This project was conducted under the International Security and Defense Policy Center of RAND's National Defense Research Institute, a federally funded research and development center sponsored by the Office of the Secretary of Defense, the Joint Staff, and the defense agencies.

CONTENTS

Preface   iii

Summary   vii

Acknowledgments   xvii

Acronyms   xix

Chapter One
    INTRODUCTION   1

PART I: CUBA IN TRANSITION

Chapter Two
    CUBA: HEADING FOR SAFE OR PERILOUS WATERS? . . .   5
    The Present Course: Signs of Safety Ahead   5
    The Present Course: Signs of Danger Ahead   14
    Present and Future Uncertainties   20

Chapter Three
    DOMESTIC FACTORS AFFECTING CUBAN OUTCOMES .   23
    Economic Reforms and Their Political Costs   24
    Political Liberalization to Regain Legitimacy   26
    The Breadth and Intensity of Regime Opposition   28
    Security Forces: Avoiding a Cuban Tiananmen   32
    Regime Cohesiveness   32

Chapter Four
    REGIME LEADERS, TENDENCIES, AND INSTITUTIONAL
        PLAYERS   35
    The Castro Dynasty   36

Policy Tendencies Within the Regime   39
Institutional Actors and the Yummies   43

Chapter Five
CIVIL SOCIETY ACTORS   53
The Catholic Church   54
Protestant Churches and Afro-Cuban Religions   56
Secular Nongovernmental Organizations   59
Implications for Cuba's Transition Process   61

PART II: U.S. POLICY AND CUBA

Chapter Six
PRESENT U.S. POLICY AND ITS OPTIONS   65
The Cuban Democracy Act of 1992   66
The Pros and Cons of the Embargo   69
The Arguments Revisited   73

Chapter Seven
U.S. POLICY OPTIONS AND CUBAN FUTURES   77
Staying the Course   77
Tightening the Embargo Under Helms-Burton   79
Lifting the Embargo   81
Assessing the Four Policies and Their Outcomes   89

Chapter Eight
A PROACTIVE POLICY FOR CUBA   93
Agents of Change and Their Paralysis   94
Orchestrating the Catalyst for Change   95
The Limitations of a Proactive Policy 100

Postscript 105

Appendix: ACTORS, MODELS, AND ENDGAMES 107
Endgame I: The Regime Muddles Through 108
Endgame II: Heightened Authoritarianism and Stasis . . . 111
Endgame III: Nonviolent Change and Power-Sharing . . . 114
Endgame IV: Violent System Change 117
Conclusions 119

Bibliography 121

CUBA'S COURSE HEADING: TOWARD SAFE OR PERILOUS WATERS?

The Castro regime has so far survived the acute economic crisis that followed the demise of the Soviet Union. The economy's free fall may have bottomed out in 1995 with the government's success in promoting foreign investments and tourism, reducing the state budget deficit, strengthening the Cuban *peso*, reforming the banking system, and reopening the farmers' markets. A new foreign-investment law could bring in additional foreign capital, although the island's antiquated and rundown transportation and communication infrastructure and its uncertain political future lessen Cuba's attractiveness to foreign investors. Meanwhile, the government predicts a 2.5-percent-or-more growth rate in gross domestic product (GDP) in 1995.

The economy's slight upturn in 1995 has given the regime greater breathing room. Political stability is further aided by Cuba's strong state—a state that is buttressed by an efficient internal security apparatus, strong regime cohesion, and residual sources of political legitimacy and mass support—and by a weak civil society. The May 2, 1995, immigration agreement with the United States has also helped dampen unrest. This past year was not marred by popular disturbances of the kind that rocked the Havana waterfront in August 1994.

However, Cuba's ship of state has yet to clear perilous waters. Much will depend on whether the island rebounds from the 1995 sugarcane harvest of only 3.3 million metric tons, the worst in 52 years, after experiencing two poor harvests in 1993 and 1994. A harvest of well over 4 million tons is needed in 1996 if Cuba is to meet its 1996 financial and trade commitments, satisfy internal demand, and generate surplus foreign-exchange earnings.

The economy's precariousness is heightened by the opposition of Castro and other hardliners to market reforms for the internal economy. Cuba is not Vietnam, with its thriving domestic market economy and private sector, which are protected by a new civil code. Castro is intent on preventing the rise of a new, independent Cuban bourgeoisie.

Two years after legalizing self-employment in 150 trades, crafts, and services, the government had licensed only 210,000 individual entrepreneurs, but with the proviso that they cannot hire nonrelatives. These mom-and-pop entrepreneurs are burdened by other onerous restrictions. Indeed, the incentives and guarantees under the new foreign-investment law apply to Cuban exiles, but not to Cuban citizens on the island.

The absence of a large market-driven domestic economy bodes ill for Cuba. To further reduce the state deficit, the government will need to start laying off some 500,000 workers from inefficient or superfluous state enterprises. Although some workers may be relocated to other state enterprises, the vast majority are likely to become unemployed, because the private sector is too small to provide jobs. And social tensions may increase, because, even at a 4.0-percent annual growth rate, Cuba would not recover to its 1989 economic levels until the year 2005.

Meanwhile, Cuba is changing as independent civil society actors emerge. The Catholic and Protestant churches, together with their respective lay groups, have attracted a wide following. A growing number of nongovernmental organizations (NGOs), some spawned initially by the state, could ultimately break free of the government. Although their members have been harassed and jailed, human-rights and dissident circles have mushroomed. Over 100 groups have joined the umbrella opposition front, *Concilio Cubano*, in pressing for government permission to hold a public forum in early 1996.

Although Cuba is in transition, a liberal, democratic state is not in sight. Instead, Cuba remains on course toward "market-Leninism," in which there are but limited market reforms and the Communist Party retains its vanguard status, monopolizing power with the support of the Army and, especially, the internal security forces. Without nationally recognized opposition leaders and feasible political alternatives, the vast majority of Cubans appear resigned to the status quo. Taken together, these factors point to stasis or, at best, limited controlled change for Cuba in the future.

Nevertheless, because civil society remains embryonic, the impetus for systemic change most likely will have to come from above, from within the regime itself. But the regime is divided into three camps, or policy tendencies, of which only one is committed to deepening Cuba's reforms:

- Fidel Castro and the *duros* (hardliners) are prepared to repress any sign of political dissent and strongly oppose the introduction of a market system. They effectively brake political and economic liberalization. The *duros* are found among the Party's old guard and the Ministry of Interior.

- Raúl Castro and his *centristas* are also hard line on security issues and oppose replacing Cuba's socialist economy with a market system. But they advocate employment of market *mechanisms* and Western managerial techniques to improve the state-run economy. They are backed by the Army, which has assumed a central role in the economy, and by the "Yummies" (young, upwardly mobile communists) who serve as technocrats, managers, and economic expediters. The centrists are behind Cuba's modest reforms.

- Foreign Minister Roberto Robaina, economic czar Carlos Lage, and, most recently, National Bank President Francisco Soberón lead the *reformistas*. They may be more willing to tolerate dissidents and a loyal opposition. They recognize the efficacy of the market system and, unlike the *centristas*, embrace a mixed economy that would include an enlarged private sector. The weakest of the three policy tendencies, the reformists are found mainly among young economists and technocrats, many of whom work in government-supported research centers.

Cuba's peaceful transition to a more open economy and polity will require ascendance of the *reformistas*, supported by a civil society.

PRESENT U.S. POLICY, POLICY ALTERNATIVES, AND CUBAN OUTCOMES

Internal actors and forces will determine the outcome of Cuba's transition process. U.S. policy may, however, help accelerate or hinder Cuba's transition by the way it (1) affects the regime's internal distribution of power, (2) provides incentives or disincentives for reform, and (3) promotes Cuba's civil society. Current U.S. policy and its options need to be assessed according to these criteria over the short term (under 1 year), medium term (1–3 years), and long term (over 3 years).

The Cuban Democracy Act

The 1992 Cuban Democracy Act (CDA), under its Track I provisions, tightened the then–30-year-old embargo to the point that Castro has made lifting it his number-one foreign-policy priority. The CDA stipulates that the embargo will be lifted once Cuba has held democratic elections, respects human rights, and moves toward a market economy. The CDA provides the U.S. Government with leverage in negotiating a future settlement of U.S. claims against the Cuban Government, and the embargo, by compounding the economy's difficulties, also helps the *centristas* and *reformistas* argue for reforms. With increased communication flows, academic and professional exchanges, and support for Cuban NGOs now being implemented under Track II of the CDA, current policy could also help open up Cuba.

On the other hand, the CDA strengthens the political hand of Castro and the hardliners over the short to medium term by enabling them to rally nationalist-minded Cubans behind the regime and to justify a garrison state. And, instead of creating divisions within the leadership, the CDA forces reformers—civilian and military—into supporting Castro.

Imperfect as it is, the CDA remains a prudent course until Cuba undergoes a deeper transformation. It does not give Castro and the hardliners a way out of their historical dilemma. It resonates with the core U.S. values concerning democracy and market economies that are now being adopted in countries throughout Latin America and the Caribbean. If the Castro regime hangs on, however, present policy may not be sustainable much beyond 1996.

The Helms-Burton Bill

Passed in two versions by the House and Senate, the Helms-Burton bill intends to speed Castro's demise by imposing punitive sanctions against foreign governments, companies, and individuals investing in and trading with Cuba, and by opposing international agencies' giving aid and loans to Cuba. Over the short to medium term, Helms-Burton would hurt the Castro regime and the Cuban people economically. It might ultimately lead to the regime's undoing—or to protracted instability and higher levels of state repression by an entrenched regime.

Even though it has not yet become law, Helms-Burton works to the political advantage of Castro and the hardliners. It provides the regime with a further pretext to crack down on dissidents and other civil society actors, and to rally Cubans against the "empire." Because the bill provides for restitution of expropriated properties for Cuban-Americans, the regime exploits the fear of permanent impoverishment among social beneficiaries of the Revolution. And it forces civil and military reformers to close ranks around the Castro brothers in the face of an immediate external threat, notwithstanding the bill's promise to provide aid to a post-Castro military.

Implementation of Helms-Burton would strain relations with U.S. allies. Were it to lead to Castro's downfall, its success would probably set back relations with Latin America and tarnish the legitimacy of post-Castro governments, as occurred in the decades following the U.S.-engineered ouster of the Arbenz government in Guatemala in 1954.

Lifting the Embargo Unconditionally

Lifting the embargo unconditionally would greatly strengthen Castro's stature within and outside the regime. He would be seen as having successfully steered Cuba's ship of state into safe waters, because the regime would now have the U.S. tourist and investment dollars with which to overcome the island's crisis without having to enact deeper reforms. Castro, the *duros*, and *centristas*—precisely those circles most opposed to economic and political liberalization—would be firmly ensconced and the *reformistas* marginalized.

For the short to medium term, this policy option would thus ensure Cuba's continuance as a market-Leninist state—in effect, a Caribbean version of Vietnam. Over the long term, it might eventually set in motion uncontrollable societal forces that would strengthen the *reformistas*. But whether democracy and a market economy would follow would depend on whether the Castro brothers were still running Cuba.

Lifting the Embargo Conditionally

Lifting the embargo on the condition that Castro hold internationally supervised elections could provide a peaceful mechanism for advancing system change. However, the feasibility of this option depends on the island's experiencing such a sharp economic deterioration that Castro has no alternative but to accept the proposed *quid pro quo*. Were Cuba to reach that point, one of two possible outcomes would occur:

Castro and the Communist Party Win. This election result would legitimize and strengthen an antidemocratic, antimarket regime. Even so, some political space would have been created for civil society, and the newly elected Castro regime might come to resemble Mexico's authoritarian regime of decades past.

Castro and the Communist Party Lose. This election outcome would put Cuba on the road toward democracy and a market-oriented economy. A more robust civil society could now begin to emerge. For an indefinite period, however, there probably would be considerable political turmoil of the kind that befell post-1990 Nicaragua: *Fidelistas* and/or *raulistas* could still control the Army, and the Communist Party could order strikes and antigovernment demonstrations.

The conditional lifting of the embargo is unrealistic. Castro will not repeat the *Sandinistas'* mistake and risk losing power through a bourgeois election when he retains control over Cuba. He underscores this point by continuing to imprison or exile dissidents, human-rights activists, and independent journalists and intellectuals.

A Proactive Policy for Cuba

Rather than adopting Helms-Burton or lifting the embargo, a bolder approach would be to maintain the embargo, or at least its ban on U.S. investments and credits and on loans from international agencies, while selectively targeting Cuba's agents of change, who are present not only in an embryonic civil society but also within the regime itself. The objective would be to induce those agents to bring about system change from above and below.

Change agents outside the regime include the Catholic and Protestant churches and their lay groups, together with students, intellectuals, artists, workers, small entrepreneurs, and dissident and human-rights groups. Those inside the regime include the regime's civilian and military *reformistas*. Together, they could become the genesis of a coalition government of national reconciliation in a post-Castro Cuba.

On the societal front, the proactive policy would expand on the U.S. efforts to strengthen civil society actors that are currently being implemented under Track II of the CDA. For example, the present onerous restrictions on humanitarian assistance distributed by Cuban NGOs could be eased. Advanced telecommunication equipment, such as cellular phones, could be licensed for marketing in Cuba. The August 1994 ban on cash remittances by Cuban-Americans could be rescinded to enable individuals and fledgling NGOs to become financially independent of the Cuban state.

A more robust civil society is needed if change from above is to be supported by change from below. The model should be Leipzig 1989, when a coalition of Lutheran pastors, reformed communists, and intellectual leaders, supported by mass demonstrations, precipitated the defection of the East German army and the collapse of the communist regime.

On the regime front, the proactive policy would employ public diplomacy to address the concerns of Cuban elites. American officials should pledge nonaggression toward Cuba, respect for the sovereignty and independence of a post-Castro Cuba, and recognition of the future role that civilian and military reformers could play in a new Cuba. Because it is a pivotal institution, the Revolutionary Armed Forces (FAR) should be singled out for special attention. The U.S. Government should lift its ban on contact between U.S. and Cuban military attachés in third countries and consider such confidence-building measures as inviting FAR observers to military exercises in the Caribbean.

To weaken Castro's hold, and perhaps hasten his departure, the United States could also publicly propose a "grand bargain" for the Cuban people. The United States would pledge not only to lift the embargo and normalize relations but also to return Guantánamo Naval Base to Cuba after Castro had left the island and after internationally supervised elections for a new government had been held. By offering the grand bargain, the United States could begin to alter the political calculus of key civilian and military actors in the regime, and among the populace at large. Ultimately, Cubans may conclude that Castro has ceased to be indispensable, that they now have a way out of Cuba's predicament, and that the *comandante* and his followers must go.

POSTSCRIPT

Since this study's completion in early December 1995, Cuban developments have taken a turn for the worse. In mid-December, Castro fired his Minister of Investments and Cooperation, Ernesto Melendez Bach, a *reformista*. Starting in mid-February 1996, some 100 members of *Concilio Cubano* were arrested by state security agents. Then, on February 24, after earlier violations of Cuban airspace and dropping of leaflets, two civilian aircraft flown by the Cuban-American humanitarian group Brothers to the Rescue were destroyed by Cuban MiGs. State repression against internal civil disobedience thus assumed an external dimension in heightened confrontation with Cuban exiles and the United States.

The White House promptly responded, not only with new sanctions but also by negotiating an agreement with Congress on the stalled Helms-Burton bill. Henceforth, the embargo will be greatly tightened and locked into law, to be lifted or eased only by Congress. A new, tougher U.S. stance toward Havana will thus complement the stasis that Cuba is virtually certain to experience during the remainder of 1996 and beyond.

ACKNOWLEDGMENTS

I wish to thank my RAND colleagues Kevin O'Connell and Tom Szayna for their constructive reviews of the earlier draft report, and David Ronfeldt for his suggestions, perceptive comments, and moral support. I am indebted to Peter Orr, Co-Chair, Inter-Agency Working Group on Support for the Cuban People, for taking the time to read the earlier draft that was distributed to some offices in the U.S. Government last September, and for sending me his written comments and observations. I also wish to thank Marian Branch for her careful, expeditious editing of the revised manuscript. The efforts of these readers notwithstanding, I alone bear responsibility for whatever errors or problems remain in the analysis, conclusions, and recommendations.

ANAP	National Association of Small Peasants
ANEIC	National Association of Independent Economists of Cuba
BPIC	Independent Press Bureau of Cuba
CDA	Cuban Democracy Act
CDR	Committees for the Defense of the Revolution
CEA	Center for the Study of America
CEE	Center for European Studies
DGCI	General Directorate of Counter-Intelligence
DGI	General Directorate of Intelligence
DIA	Defense Intelligence Agency
EMI	Military Industrial Enterprise
FAR	Revolutionary Armed Forces
FMC	Federation of Cuban Women
GDP	Gross domestic product
KGB	Komitet Gosudarstvennoi Bezopasnosti (Soviet Secret Police)
MINFAR	Ministry of Revolutionary Armed Forces
MININT	Ministry of Interior
MTT	Territorial Troop Militia
NGO	Nongovernmental organization
PCC	Communist Party of Cuba
PRI	Institutional Revolutionary Party (Mexico)
UN	United Nations
UNEAC	Union of Writers and Artists
Yummies	Young, upwardly mobile communists

Chapter One

INTRODUCTION

The collapse of the Soviet Union and the devastating economic crisis that followed in Cuba led many observers to believe that it would be only a matter of time before the island would shed its 37-year-old communist dictatorship and move toward a post-Castro future. Some recent studies have speculated about what a "free Cuba" would look like;[1] others have proposed a "road map" for improving relations with a post-Castro Cuba.[2] But most do not spell out an endgame, or *how* Cuba is to "get there from here"—in other words, how Cuba's Leninist regime and state-controlled economy might evolve into something else, or how and why the regime would be replaced by a democratic government committed to a market economy.[3]

The 1994 RAND report *Storm Warnings for Cuba* analyzed where Cuba was headed, developed endgames and assigned them probabilities, then offered policy recommendations for dealing with differ-

---

[1]For a recent example, see Bryan T. Johnson and John P. Sweeney, "A Blueprint for a Free Cuba," *The Heritage Foundation Backgrounder*, March 23, 1995.

[2]See the consensus document developed by the Working Group of The Atlantic Council of the United States, *A Road Map for Restructuring Future U.S. Relations with Cuba*, Washington, D.C., June 1995.

[3]The major exception is the Inter-American Dialogue, *Cuba in the Americas: Breaking the Policy Deadlock*, Washington, D.C.: The Second Report of the Inter-American Dialogue Task Force in Cuba, September 1995, which prescribes a series of key policy changes by both the United States and Cuba in order to achieve an accommodation between the two countries. Composed of public- and private-sector leaders from the United States and Latin America, the Dialogue seeks to promote closer relations between the two Americas.

ent Cuban outcomes.[4] These remain the tasks for the present study, which builds on the earlier analysis. However, this study employs a different analytical lens and focus, and it outlines a new proactive policy for hastening the process of change in Cuba by outflanking Castro.

The study begins in Part I by presenting two different snapshots of present-day Cuba—one suggesting that the regime is on a course to survival, the other suggesting that the regime could still founder in the months or years ahead. It next identifies the key domestic variables that are likely to determine Cuba's future course over the short term (within 1 year) and medium term (between 1 and 3 years). It then looks at the regime's leadership, policy tendencies, and principal institutions, and at signs that civil society actors may be emerging outside the regime, and concludes by assessing their likely roles in Cuba's current and future transition scenarios.

Part II focuses on U.S. policy toward a Cuba in transition. It first examines the goals and assumptions underlying the Cuban Democracy Act, which is the basis for current policy, and the alternative options of tightening the embargo under the Helms-Burton bill or of lifting the embargo, conditionally and unconditionally. It next assesses the effect of each of these policies on key regime players and civil society actors in Cuba, and whether each policy will hasten or retard peaceful change over the short to longer term. Part II concludes by outlining measures that the United States could pursue under a bolder, proactive policy for promoting Cuba's transition to a democratic polity and market-driven economy.

Finally, the Appendix projects alternative endgames for Castro's Cuba in the absence of a proactive U.S. policy and assesses the implications of each endgame for the United States. Of the four endgames that are presented, one depicts a Cuba that is in a controlled-crisis mode, as it now is; the other three revolve around a Cuba that is overtaken by uncontrolled-crisis situations.

---

[4]See Edward Gonzalez and David Ronfeldt, *Storm Warnings for Cuba,* Santa Monica, Calif.: RAND, MR-452-OSD, 1994. Prepared for the Office of the Under Secretary of Defense for Policy, the report was completed in June 1994 and released that August.

PART I: CUBA IN TRANSITION

Chapter Two

CUBA: HEADING FOR SAFE OR PERILOUS WATERS?

Despite having been set adrift in a postcommunist world, and despite its uncertain, at times zig-zag course in recent years, Cuba's ship of state remains afloat. The Castro regime has so far weathered the worst economic crisis in its 37 years, a crisis produced by the disappearance of the Soviet Union. Now, 1996 may be the decisive year in which the Cuban ship of state, with Fidel Castro at the helm, clears perilous waters or finally begins to go aground.

THE PRESENT COURSE: SIGNS OF SAFETY AHEAD

Fidel and Raúl Castro and their followers are trying to avoid the mistakes that led to the demise of the East European and Soviet regimes. They are doing so by steering Cuba's ship of state toward "market-Leninism," an economic and political system similar to what has emerged in China and especially in Vietnam. Cuba's market-Leninist model combines a limited form of economic liberalism, tightly directed and controlled by the state, with political authoritarianism under the leadership of Cuba's vanguard Communist Party.

Cuba's Strong State

In the political realm, the Castro regime retains its exclusive lock on political power and tolerates little public criticism, much less organized opposition to the monopoly of power exercised by the Communist Party of Cuba (PCC). The PCC and the Ministry of Interior (MININT) channel political behavior and repress dissent using various mechanisms of social control, ranging from informers,

5

secret police, and Rapid Reaction Brigades (goon squads), to the forced expatriation of dissidents and human-rights activists, to the permanent exile abroad of those dissidents and activists as a condition for release from prison.

The regime's strength does not reside solely in the coercive instruments of state power, however. Its strength also stems from the residue of popular legitimacy that the regime still enjoys among some sectors of the populace and from the loyalty and commitment of Party, government, and security personnel, who retain a strong stake in the existing system. Although less powerful than in decades past, Cuba thus continues to have a strong state that confronts a weak, embryonic civil society represented chiefly by the independent, but ever-cautious, Catholic Church and other religious groups.

Economic Reforms, Cuban Style

The major changes produced by Cuba's current transition process have occurred in its economic system. Cuba no longer has the closed command economy of the past, because the regime has made efforts to integrate the island into the world economy. Although the state remains the dominant actor, Cuba's economy has become bifurcated in recent years, with different systems operating in the external and internal economies.

External Economy. In the external (foreign-exchange-producing) sector of the economy, the government allows both foreign firms and the market[1] to operate in ways that attract foreign capital, optimize foreign-exchange earnings, and meet energy requirements. The government has thus opened the island to foreign investors in tourism, mining, petroleum exploration, biotechnology, and, most recently, nuclear-energy and sugar financing and marketing. Between 1990

---

[1]A *market economy* is an economic system in which production and exchange activities are driven primarily by forces of supply and demand and by profit considerations, with free prices serving as the principal mechanism for allocating resources. Generally, the major share of productive property is under private or autonomous ownership in a market economy. Such a system stands in contrast to Cuba's command economy, aspects of which still remain operative, where most sectors of the economy were subject to central planning and price-setting by the state, and where state ownership and control of the economy prevailed except in the illegal black market.

and 1994, the cumulative level of these investments was reported at $1.5 billion. In many of these areas, the government has established enterprises under joint foreign and Cuban ownership. However, Cuban owners and managers are state-appointed loyalists drawn from the ranks of the Party, the Ministry of Interior, and the Army.

On September 5, 1995, the National Assembly approved a new foreign-investment law that the government hopes will provide the incentives for attracting needed venture capital from the international business community. Among the most important provisions are those that

- allow full ownership of business by foreigners without participation by a Cuban investor, as required in the past

- create free-trade zones, providing preferential treatment in exchange rates, custom duties, taxes, etc., for foreign import and export facilities, warehouses, assembly plants, and reexport activities

- permit foreigners to own real estate (except land)

- provide foreign firms with hard currency for expropriated properties

- compensate foreign investors for assets claimed by third parties (i.e., in the United States) that were expropriated by the Cuban state in the first years of the Revolution, provided such claims have been recognized by the state (none have been so far)

- permit Cuban exiles (but not Cubans residing on the island) to also invest in new ventures.[2]

One concession that had earlier been rumored but that the National Assembly did not adopt would have allowed foreign business to hire and pay workers directly. Under the new law, companies will continue to employ workers who are selected and paid through state hiring agencies. This arrangement enables the Cuban state to reap a bonanza of hard currency and, in the process, to exploit Cuban labor.

---

[2]"New Investment Law Debated: Would Widen Opportunities," *CubaNews*, August 1995, p. 5; and "Cuba: Text of Foreign Investment Law," *FBIS-LAT-95-193-S*, October 5, 1995, pp. 1–11.

According to Toronto's *Globe and Mail*, for example, Sherritt, Inc., the Canadian mining company, pays the Cuban government an average of $9,500 per year for each of the 1,720 Cuban workers it employs through the state employment agency. How much does the Cuban worker get? One university graduate employed at Sherritt's Moa nickel mine gets about $10 per month from the state agency, and only 9.0 to 12.0 percent of that amount is in dollars.[3]

While the new law is a radical departure for Cuba, it may not be sufficient to entice long-term investment capital, particularly in manufacturing. In assessing Cuba's investment opportunities relative to those of other countries, foreign investors must take into account Cuba's antiquated and run-down transportation and communication infrastructure, government hiring laws, lack of an internal market economy, and uncertainties surrounding the Castro government's policies and longevity. Still, the new law's concessions to foreign capital, including opening the door to Cuban exiles, indicate that the regime realizes it must do more to attract foreign investors.

Internal Economy. On the other hand, some things have not changed all that much. The government keeps in place its own "third embargo"—a term used in private by the leadership to refer to the regime's stance against the rise of a large Cuban-owned private sector. Thus, the new investment law applies to Cuban exiles but not to Cuban citizens in Cuba, an incongruity that Castro had problems justifying in the National Assembly.[4] The state also retains control over who can be employed by foreign corporations.

Cuba's internal economy has witnessed far less liberalization than has the external sector. The regime feels more secure in managing the state's transactions with a few hundred Canadian, European, and

---

[3]Paul Knox, "Sherritt Breathes Life into Cuban Mine," *Globe and Mail*, July 31, 1995. p. B6.

[4]A National Assembly deputy asked Castro why "should there be two types of Cubans? The Cuban who emigrates and the Cuban who remains here?" Castro replied that the exclusion of Cuban exiles would be seen abroad as "something strange" and therefore disquieting to other potential foreign investors. He insisted that "nobody should believe that the investments will pour into this country," and that the government would carefully assess investment proposals by exiles. He further justified the law's discrimination on grounds that Cubans residing in Cuba could not "contribute to what we are seeking abroad: capital, technology, and markets." See *FBIS-LAT-95-173-S*, September 7, 1995, pp. 6, 8, 9.

Latin American corporations than in coping with a new social class composed of hundreds of thousands of independent private Cuban entrepreneurs.

Hence, the government has enacted only a few market-type measures for the internal economy, and these only grudgingly, to ease the extreme austerity experienced by Cubans. Even so, the regime has been careful to prevent the reemergence of a large, legalized private sector—i.e., a domestic bourgeoisie—that could assert its independence and challenge the regime's authority. For example, under Decree 141, which was enacted in fall 1993, the Cuban Government permits "self-employment" activities in about 150 trades, crafts, and services, on condition that nonrelatives not be hired, while also imposing other onerous restrictions, such as on the number of tables allowed in home restaurants.

The regime's opposition to a market-driven economy was made clear by Castro in his strident July 26, 1995, speech commemorating the forty-second anniversary of his assault on the Moncada barracks, the opening volley of the Cuban Revolution. In it, he reaffirmed his Marxist-Leninist convictions and rejected capitalism as an option. He cited the path taken by China and Vietnam as showing the way that socialism and the Revolution could be saved in Cuba.

Although the regime looks favorably on the Vietnamese model, the depth and breadth of Cuba's economic liberalization lag those of Vietnam. In Vietnam, as in Cuba, the state retains overall direction of the economy and has opened the country to foreign investors. But unlike Cuba, Hanoi permits a flourishing internal market economy, consisting of small farms, shops, cafes, small manufacturing firms, and other private-sector activities run by Vietnamese. Despite the heavy hand of the bureaucracy, these activities are now protected by a recently adopted civil code, and they have helped transform the country.[5]

In contrast, save for the foreign enclaves that are present on the island, Cuba remains very much a state-controlled economy. Only since 1993 has it begun to incorporate the type of internal economic "reforms" that were first seen in Eastern Europe starting in the 1960s.

---

[5]See Stanley Karnow, "Vietnam Now," *Smithsonian,* January 1996, pp. 32–42.

In fact, by fall 1995, only 210,000 Cubans had been licensed to become self-employed under the decree passed two years earlier.

Nevertheless, Cuba's combination of tight authoritarian rule and partial, state-directed economic liberalization has enabled the regime thus far to ride out and contain the political tensions produced by the economy's virtual free fall. While it has used coercion to limit popular discontent, the leadership has also taken steps to ameliorate conditions that originally contributed to earlier unrest.

Political and Economic Course Corrections

On August 5, 1994, the regime's security organs put down the riots that erupted on the Havana waterfront. The subsequent departure from the island of over 30,000 desperate Cubans and the new migration accord reached between Havana and Washington that September momentarily helped the regime stabilize the internal political situation. Later that same month, Raúl Castro announced that in October the government would start implementing some long-awaited reforms to ameliorate the shortage of food and consumer goods. The most important of those reforms was the decision to reopen the farmers' markets that had been closed by Castro in 1986, which has since helped ease the country's food crisis.

Meanwhile, during 1995, the government succeeded in instilling greater fiscal discipline and reducing inflationary pressures through policies that testify to the strength of the Cuban state. Those policies included charging much higher prices for such nonessential consumer goods as cigarettes, tobacco, and alcohol; assessing higher rates for fuel, electricity, public transportation, and other basic services; and imposing a sales tax on the new private markets. The government froze wages and salaries in the state sector of the economy, eliminated redundant government and Party offices, and downsized the military. It took steps to remove some 2.7 billion excess *pesos* from circulation and reduce subsidies to state enterprises, thereby reducing state deficit spending to a projected 5 percent of gross domestic product (GDP) for 1995 (compared with 8 percent in 1994).[6] These measures helped to dampen inflationary pressures.

In addition, the government began buying up dollars to ensure a better exchange rate for the state.[7] By spring 1995, the value of the Cuban *peso* had stabilized at 35–40 to the dollar compared with 100 to the dollar in 1994. By early September, the prevailing rate for the *peso* was 25 to the dollar, with the government establishing currency-exchange houses the following month that are authorized to purchase, but not to sell, dollars for *pesos*.[8]

Together with the continued opening up of the island to foreign investors, these latest reforms have eased some of the extreme austerity of recent years. In August 1995, a *New York Times* reporter observed that electrical blackouts in Havana had been reduced from as long as 12 hours a day in summer 1994 to only 8 hours a week. This improvement, together with the regime's modest economic reforms, had helped dissipate public discontent:

> Some Havana streets where Cubans had offered a symphony of complaints now buzz with snack vendors, bicycle repair shops and small, family-run restaurants. Farmers' markets that were legalized last fall do brisk business in everything from piglets and goats to snake oils and spaghetti sauce.[9]

Meanwhile, Cuba was spared damage from the 1995 hurricane season, which should help the 1996 sugar industry recover from the disastrous 1995 harvest.

---

[6]Business Monitor International, Ltd., *Latin American Monitor (Caribbean)*, November 1995, p. 6.

[7]Based on his April 1995 visit, a Freedom House specialist on Latin America reported that the government had eased up on black-market kingpins (*macetas*) or had placed Ministry of Interior agents in black-market operations, to control the exchange rate, soak up dollars for the state, and present a picture of improved financial stability to the outside world. See Douglas W. Payne, "Castro's Currency Racket," *Cuba Brief*, Washington, D.C.: Freedom House, June 1995, p. 6.

[8]*CubaNews*, November 1995, p. 3.

[9]Tim Golden, "A Year After Exodus, Threat to Castro Fades," *The New York Times*, August 15, 1995, p. 1.

A Brighter Outlook for the Future

As 1995 progressed, Cuban officials became increasingly optimistic about the economy's growth. Earlier in the year, Carlos Lage, Cuba's economic czar, had reported that the island's economic free fall had been halted in 1994 by the posting of a slight growth in GDP of 0.7 percent over that of the previous year. Then, in his July 26, 1995, speech, Castro claimed that the GDP had grown by 2.0 percent during the first half of 1995.[10] Three months later, Lage reported a 2.3-percent growth in gross domestic product. In early November, Economic and Planning Minister José Luis Rodríguez predicted a 2.5-percent growth for all of 1995, but Castro then topped this figure with a 2.7-percent growth in GDP. Still another official later predicted GDP would grow by over 3.0 percent in 1995.[11] Although the government's optimistic forecasts have usually proven unreliable in the past, particularly when proclaimed by Castro and other political leaders, these latest predictions appear to have some basis in fact.[12]

Developments on the foreign front also brightened the regime's prospects during the last quarter of 1995. In New York to attend the fiftieth anniversary of the founding of the United Nations last October, Castro was hosted not only by left-wing circles but also by leading members of the U.S. foreign policy and financial establishments. The Council on Foreign Relations, the editorial boards of *The New York Times* and *The Wall Street Journal*, David Rockefeller, and other luminaries from the financial, business, and media world heard the Cuban president hold out prospects of investment opportunities in Cuba if the U.S. embargo were lifted. Afterwards, five major American newspapers published editorials that questioned the need

---

[10]"Fidel Castro Speaks at Moncada Ceremony," *FBIS-LAT-95-145*, July 28, 1995, p. 6.

[11]"Economic Growth," *CubaNews*, December 1995, p. 6.

[12]Carmelo Mesa-Lago, the leading U.S. economist on Cuba, points out that the Cuban Government has failed to issue statistical series data on the economy since 1989. Also, he believes that the government itself has no accurate fix on the state of the economy, because the state sector is shrinking whereas the informal (nonreporting) economy has been growing. See Mesa-Lago, "Cuba's Economic Recovery—How Good Are Those 1995 Predictions?" in *Cuba Brief*, June 1995, pp. 1–2. As 1995 came to a close, however, reports from Cuba indicated that, under the prodding of Central Bank President Francisco Soberón, the government is now committed to developing and issuing a more reliable database. See "Optimism Produces Economic Disclosure," *CubaNews*, December 1995, p. 6.

for an embargo against Cuba in a postcommunist world. And a *Time* magazine delegation made up of some 50 top American executives arrived in Havana to take a first-hand look at business opportunities in Cuba.

A new three-year trade agreement, concluded in Havana the same month, provides improved terms and longer-range stability for Cuba's trade ties with Russia. Under this latest pact, Cuba will supply Russia with 1.5 million tons of raw sugar in 1996 and 1997, and 1.75 million in 1998, in exchange for 4.5 million tons of petroleum products in 1996 and 1997, and 5 million tons in 1998.[13] The pact thus goes a long way toward meeting the island's minimum energy needs, provided that both countries, each with its struggling economy, are able to live up to their respective commitments.

The sugar-oil agreement was accompanied by other, lesser agreements between Cuba and Russia, including letters of intent to improve economic cooperation in trade, transportation, basic industry, oil-refinery modernization, and development of local oil production, refining capacity, and pipelines. Russia also agreed to the continuation of a $30-million credit to enable the Cubans to maintain the unfinished Juragua nuclear plant. However, the plant cannot be completed without Western financing, which appears a remote possibility. Discussions on military cooperation between the two countries were believed to have focused on Cuba's dire need for replacement parts for its inventory of Soviet weaponry, but no agreement was announced.[14]

The new agreements reflect the economic interdependence of both countries, especially Cuba's need for Russian oil and Russia's dependence on Cuban sugar. From the Castro regime's perspective, however, the improved economic ties may be the harbinger of renewed political, ideological, and military interest in Cuba by Moscow. This renewal might occur in the future if Russia follows the trend found in some former East European bloc countries, and if the old Communists and ultranationalists score major gains in Russia's par-

---

[13]"Russia, Cuba Sign Economic Pacts," *CubaNews*, November 5, 1995, p. 5.

[14]"Russia, Cuba," 1995, p. 5; and "Trade Deals Signed with Moscow," *Latin American Monitor (Caribbean)*, Vol. 12, No. 11, November 1995, p. 5.

liamentary elections in mid-December and go on to contest the presidential elections scheduled for June 1996.[15]

As of late 1995, therefore, rank-and-file Cubans could find some encouraging signs that the worst was now behind them and that the economy was finally on its way to a slow recovery. For their part, Cuban leaders not only appeared confident that they could hang on but also that events—including those in the United States—were beginning to move in the regime's favor. As Larry Rohter of *The New York Times* reported from Havana in mid-November, Castro and his followers were now upbeat about the future:

> Fidel Castro seems to have a new spring in his step since returning from his recent visit to New York and the United Nations, and his brightened outlook has quickly percolated through the state and party apparatus that has always taken its cues from him. After enduring his six worst years since his revolution swept him into power nearly 37 years ago, Mr. Castro and his Government once again seem to be directing, rather than reacting to, events.[16]

THE PRESENT COURSE: SIGNS OF DANGER AHEAD

Despite the hopeful signs, Cuba's ship of state is by no means out of dangerous waters. The implosion of communism in the Soviet Union cost Cuba its international support system and has taken a heavy toll on the Cuban economy over the past five years. Deprived of Soviet subsidies and supportive trade ties, the island's economy contracted by over 50 percent between 1989 and 1994. This contraction and the regime's reluctance to deepen the reform process have

---

[15]Starting in 1994, former Communists have won or gained a plurality in parliamentary elections in every East European country except the Czech Republic. The ex-Communist Aleksander Kwasniewski even ousted Lech Walesa from the Polish presidency in November 1995. However, these former Communists, especially in Poland and Hungary, are different from the old-line authoritarian Communists found in Russia. Representing a younger generation of leaders, they are essentially Social Democrats who have accepted political democracy and a market-driven economy. Hence, their return to power should have little effect on the postcommunist reform process in these countries.

[16]Larry Rohter, "A Little Hope Pumps Up an Attitude," *The New York Times*, November 19, 1995, p. E3.

left the economy in a precarious, vulnerable state at a time when the regime's control over society is weakening.

An Uncertain Halt to the Economy's Free Fall

Starting in the early 1990s, severe shortages in Soviet fuel, spare parts, fertilizer, and other needed inputs sent the Cuban economy into a tailspin. In 1993 and 1994, Cuba experienced its worst back-to-back sugar harvests in over 30 years when production dropped to 4.28 and 4.0 million metric tons, respectively, compared with the 7.5-to-7.7-million-ton harvests during the 1980s. These harvest shortfalls decimated the island's foreign-exchange earnings, leading to further reductions in fuel and other critical imports needed for agriculture and industry. As a consequence, in 1993 and 1994, "up to 80 percent of the island's factories stood idle, because of a lack of fuel, raw materials, machinery, and spare parts."[17]

The effects of this economic free fall were cumulative. The 1995 sugar harvest dropped below the shortfalls of the previous two years, to only 3.3 million metric tons, the lowest harvest in 52 years. To prevent the 1995 harvest from dipping even further, the government may have also set back the 1996 harvest by apparently milling immature sugar-cane stalks that had been planted for 1996.[18] In any event, despite new cash incentives in the form of dollar certificates to the workforce,[19] the 1996 harvest is likely to continue facing major production bottlenecks that stem in large part from Cuba's 156 antiquated mills and inadequate transport. As of November 1995, the

---

[17]Jorge P. Pérez-López, "Castro Tries Survival Strategy," *Transition—The Newsletter About Reforming Economies*, Washington, D.C.: The World Bank, Vol. 6, No. 3, March 1995, p. 11. Pérez-López further points out that Cuba's exports fell by 69 percent between 1989 and 1993, whereas imports fell by 75 percent. As imports shrank, the relative share represented by imports of crude oil and petroleum products increased, which meant steep cuts were made in imports of consumer goods, raw materials, and machinery.

[18]Because the milling for the 1995 harvest was extended into late June, well beyond the norm, there was speculation that some of the sugar cane for the 1996 harvest had been cut in order to limit the 1995 shortfall.

[19]Dollar certificates can be used in state-run stores that accept only hard currency.

harvest was expected to be in the range of 3.8 to 4.5 million tons, according to outside experts.[20]

Unless the harvest is well over 4 million tons, Cuba will find it virtually impossible to meet its international financial and trade obligations, satisfy minimal domestic-consumption needs, and have sufficient sugar left to generate additional export earnings. In 1996, Cuba may need upwards of 1 million tons of sugar at current world prices to repay the European banks and trading firms that granted $116–$123 million in loans, at 8-percent interest, to eight of the country's top sugar-producing provinces. The loans were to help Cuba finance fertilizer and pesticide imports and to market what had been expected to be a banner sugar crop.

In the meantime, Cuba has yet to make delivery to Russia on the 1 million tons of raw sugar, owed under the 1995 agreement, that is due by March 1996. Cuba must also supply China with the balance of 250,000 tons under a 1995 agreement, although this commitment may have been eased during Castro's visit to China in December. In addition, as noted earlier, Cuba is committed to exporting 1.5 million tons of raw sugar to Russia in 1996 under the latest agreement, in exchange for 4.5 million tons of Russian petroleum products.[21] These commitments alone run to a total of 3.75 million tons for 1996.

According to Carmelo Mesa-Lago, the leading U.S. specialist on the Cuban economy, the growing tourist industry has not offset the loss in sugar revenues. A record number of 630,000 tourists from Canada, Europe, and Latin America visited the island in 1994, yielding $850 million in gross revenues. But Cuba gained only an estimated $255 million in net profits because of the cost of imports, commissions, and various fees needed to run the tourist industry.[22] As of October 1995, the government was predicting an increase of 90,000 more

---

[20]In its September quarterly report, the London-based International Sugar Organization said the Cuba could produce 4.5 million tons in 1996. However, British traders and statisticians E. D. & F. Man, who monitor Cuban production directly in the field, predicted a 3.8-million-ton harvest. "Experts Expect Better Harvest, Not Full Recovery," *CubaNews*, November 1995, p. 6. See also Larry Rohter, "Cuba Gambles on Reversing Fall in Sugar Harvest," *The New York Times*, November 26, 1995, p. 3.

[21]See "Sugar Harvest Committed," *CubaNews*, October 1995, p. 5; and "Russia, Cuba," *CubaNews*, 1995, p. 5.

[22]Mesa-Lago, "Cuba's Economic Recovery," *Cuba Brief*, 1995, p. 2.

tourists over 1994, for a total of 720,000 in 1995.[23] Even so, net profits probably will not exceed $300 million.

An Impending Unemployment Problem

Meanwhile, to reduce large budget deficits and inflationary pressures, the government may eventually have to lay off upwards of 500,000 employees working in inefficient state enterprises, two-thirds of which must be subsidized. Initially, the layoffs were expected to be implemented over a 12-month period, perhaps starting in fall 1995. Workers were to receive one month of severance pay plus 60 percent of their former monthly wages until they find new employment. As of the beginning of December, the government had been able to postpone the layoffs. Sooner or later, however, the downsizing will need to be implemented. It will necessitate a further increase in social-security expenditures, which already accounted for 68 percent of the 1995 state budget.[24]

The government will try to relocate laid-off workers to other areas of the economy in which labor shortages exist. The problem is that urban workers may not want to accept lower-paying, less-attractive agricultural work or to move to where housing, services, and other amenities are inadequate.[25] Meanwhile, laid-off workers will swell the rolls of the unemployed or underemployed, which independent Cuban economists put at nearly 52 percent of the labor force in 1995, or over 3.2 million men and women.[26]

The laid-off workers are not likely to be absorbed by Cuba's legalized private sector, which remains small and hamstrung by the state. Castro made clear his opposition to a domestic private sector in a discussion with a delegation from *Time* magazine in February 1995:

---

[23]"Deputy Tourism Minister Notes Sector Development," *FBIS-LAT-95-202*, October 19, 1995, p. 27.

[24]*CubaNews*, June 1995, p. 2.

[25]*CubaNews*, June 1995, p. 2.

[26]"Nada que echar la javita," by Marta Beatriz Roque Cabello, Member of the National Association of Independent Economists of Cuba (ANEIC), Havana, via e-mail on CubaNet, April 5, 1995.

> . . . we are not implementing a privatization policy. For domestic consumption, we prefer our own industries . . . [and] we prefer that they continue being state-owned. We have no interest in privatizing domestic enterprises. We won't renounce the fundamental role of the state in the development of the economy.[27]

Accordingly, the government has not loosened its restrictions on self-employment. Instead, it has enacted only half-measures, some of which took away as much as they gave.

Thus, in early summer 1995, the government added some new self-employment categories to the list, announced that university-trained professionals may now be self-employed, and legalized the *paladares* (home restaurants). But these "reforms" continued the ban on the hiring of nonrelatives by the self-employed; prohibited university-trained professionals from self-employment in their respective academic specialties; and limited the *paladares* to 12 tables each while also imposing steep monthly fees that may drive many out of existence.[28]

In late November, the government announced that it would begin to collect personal income taxes on hard-currency earners, starting January 1, 1996. A minimum tax level of 10 percent is set on annual incomes of up to $2,400, with a maximum tax of 50 percent on incomes of more than $60,000. For now, the new taxes are aimed at Cuba's new "dollar class"—those working in tourism and foreign businesses, along with artists, musicians, intellectuals, athletes, and professionals who travel and work abroad, and obtain hard-currency earnings—but new taxes on *peso* income earned by self-employed workers are also due later on. The tax collections are needed, the

---

[27]"Castro's Compromises," *Time*, February 20, 1995, p. 58.

[28]The same bias against private economic activity exists in agriculture, where the number of small private farms declined by 16,000 in the past seven years. According to official Cuban statistics, there were only 102,000 small private farms left in Cuba in 1988 (see A.R.M. Ritter, *Exploring Cuba's Alternative Economic Futures*, Ottawa, Canada: Carleton University, The Norman Paterson School of International Affairs, Development Studies Working Paper, No. 4, 1992, p. 10). In 1995, the President of the National Bank of Cuba reported that the number of small farms had declined still further to 86,000. He claimed that, prior to the 1993 reforms, agriculture had been dominated by 300 state farms, whereas more than 4,000 cooperatives, together with the 86,000 small farms, now controlled 73 percent of Cuba's cultivable land. ("Why Change Is Needed," *CubaNews*, December 1995, p. 2.)

government maintains, so that it can continue financing the social programs that benefit the entire population.[29] Whether this latest fiscal reform is also intended to curb and control private entrepreneurial activity or is a prelude to opening up the internal economy to private-sector activity remains to be seen.

In the meantime, these obstructions and restrictions have rendered the legalized private sector in trade, crafts, and services—composed mostly of 210,000 mom-and-pop ventures—too minuscule to absorb those unemployed workers who are to be laid off from state enterprises. The scale of these firms—as opposed to state-sponsored joint enterprises in the external sector of the economy—remains much smaller than many of the private establishments that were in operation in Cuba prior to Castro's wholesale nationalization of some 65,000 firms in 1968.

The magnitude of this impending unemployment problem is further compounded when Cuba's modest economic recovery of 2.5-percent growth in GDP in 1995 is put in perspective: *Even if the economy were to attain an annual growth rate of 4.0 percent, Cuba would still have to wait until the year 2005 before 1989 economic levels were restored.* Thus, unless far-reaching reforms are enacted and lead to significant economic growth and expansion, rising social tensions are likely to await Cuba in the not-too-distant future.

The Changing Nature of Cuban Society

Even as it remains intent on blocking the reemergence of a bourgeoisie, and preserving socialism in the process, the regime's control over society is weakening. With the support of the Protestant and Catholic churches, especially the latter, workers, academics, and others are forming self-help groups and budding nongovernmental organizations (NGOs) that are beginning to engage in social and political activities independent of the state. Although still behind Eastern Europe in this regard, such groups could provide the basis for the eventual development of civil society, which could begin to challenge the regime. As a Catholic lay worker recently told a *Wall*

---

[29]See "Income Taxes Introduced" and "Tax Will Hit Elite Hardest," *CubaNews*, January 1996, p. 2.

Street Journal correspondent in June 1995, "It's a total error to think that Cuba is just the Castro government. It's not that way anymore."[30]

Indeed, although harassed and frequently jailed, the regime's political opponents are now becoming braver—even audacious—in pressing for a more open, democratic political system. In early December, *Concilio Cubano* (Cuban Council), a broad political alliance made up of over 100 human-rights and dissident groups committed to bringing about peaceful democratic change, announced its plan to convene a national meeting in Havana in late January 1996. Although two of its leaders were arrested, *Concilio Cubano* told reporters that it would request that the government provide it with a meeting place where it can deliberate and propose necessary political changes to move Cuba toward democracy.[31]

PRESENT AND FUTURE UNCERTAINTIES

As these two different views of present-day Cuba suggest, the signs are mixed on where the country is headed. Since *Storm Warnings for Cuba* was completed in June 1994, Cuban society has been changing, even though the emergence of a strong civil society remains distant. The regime continues its cautious course of enacting only a few, modest economic reforms. Save for the farmers' market and a few other minor reforms, the "third embargo" on the marketization of the domestic economy remains pretty much in place.

Nonetheless, the government has now instilled greater fiscal discipline in the state-run economy, reduced inflation and money in circulation, and attracted some additional foreign investments. There are thus some grounds for believing that the economy may be on the rebound. Still, the economic situation remains precarious, given the large-scale layoffs that may lie ahead, the obstacles facing the 1996 sugar harvest, and the resulting uncertainties regarding Cuba's ability to meet its financial and trade commitments.

---

[30]Carla Anne Robbins, "Civics Lessons—As Economy Struggles, Cubans Find a Crack in Castro's Control," *The Wall Street Journal*, June 19, 1995, p. A4.

[31]Pablo Alfonso, "Cita en La Habana de coalición disidente," *El Nuevo Herald* (Supplement to *The Miami Herald*), December 6, 1995, pp. 1A, 8A.

Meanwhile, by the end of 1995, the government's modest success in improving living conditions had reduced social tensions from their explosive level of the previous year. This success, and the May 1995 immigration agreement with the United States that provided for more orderly out-migration, made the internal political situation much less volatile than in summer 1994. For their part, Cubans appeared resigned to the existing order and unwilling to confront a regime that remained as authoritarian as ever.

As 1995 ended, however, Cuba still remained in a controlled-crisis mode because of the economy's precariousness. Time will tell whether Cuba's relatively strong state will be sufficient to enable the regime to keep the lid on a society that is changing, particularly if deeper reforms are not forthcoming and the economy once again falters.

Chapter Three

DOMESTIC FACTORS AFFECTING CUBAN OUTCOMES

The Havana riots on August 5, 1994, the most serious faced by the Castro regime in its 35-year history, had been preceded by a contracting economy, rising social tensions, and a dramatic increase in the number of *balseros* (rafters) fleeing the island. After the disturbance was put down, Castro ordered his Border Troops on August 12 to stop preventing the rafters from fleeing Cuban shores. The exodus that followed—by nearly 35,000 men, women, and children in makeshift rafts and rickety boats—was not fully stemmed until after Washington and Havana hammered out a joint agreement on immigration on September 9, 1994.[1]

By spring 1995, despite some signs of improvements in living conditions, another hot summer of discontent appeared inevitable. By the end of April, in fact, 500 *balseros* had already fled the island. However, the latest (May 2, 1995) immigration agreement between the United States and Cuba prevented another massive outflow. Reversing past U.S. policy, the U.S. Coast Guard was ordered to return *balseros* to the Cuban Government so that they could apply for lawful immigration into the United States through the U.S. Interests Section in Havana.

The new agreement has helped the regime stabilize the internal situation. By providing for the orderly migration to the United States of a minimum of 20,000 approved Cuban applicants per year, the

---

[1]For a fuller discussion of events before and after the immigration crisis, see Max J. Castro, *Cuba: The Continuing Crisis*, Miami: University of Miami, The North-South Agenda, North-South Center, April 1995.

agreement discourages the illegal departures that the police and Border Guards had tried to prevent, at times brutally and with tragic consequences, to the detriment of the regime's international image. Moreover, the emigration lottery that the U.S. Interests Section held in 1995 further serves as a deterrent to illegal departures and civil disobedience. The lottery gives a chance of emigration to people who otherwise would be ineligible because they do not have relatives in the United States. Meanwhile, even non-winners have an incentive to continue to conform politically because their 1995 lottery numbers are to be included in the 1996 lottery.

On the other hand, the immigration agreement does close a major escape valve that desperate Cubans had used in the past, sometimes on a larger scale. Nearly 125,000 left through the port of Mariel after Castro opened the floodgates in 1980; when he again allowed Cubans to leave in August 1994, the number of *balseros* grew to 35,000 and would have gone far higher had not President Clinton sealed off U.S. shores to the rafters. But if conditions were to worsen now, Castro would find it difficult to break the new agreement, because such an action would probably trigger internal unrest, tarnish his regime's international image and credibility, and harm tourism to the island.

In any event, more-orderly out-migration is not a permanent solution to Cuba's economic and political crisis. Whether Cuba remains stable or begins to experience political instability on a scale larger than the August 5, 1994, disturbances will hinge largely on several key domestic variables. Among the most important are the pace, extent, and success of economic reforms, the willingness of the regime to relegitimize itself through political liberalization, the breadth and intensity of anti-regime sentiment, the effectiveness and reliability of the internal security forces and the military, and the regime's continued cohesiveness in the months and years ahead.

ECONOMIC REFORMS AND THEIR POLITICAL COSTS

To put Cuba on the road to economic recovery, the regime needs to accelerate the marketization and privatization of key sectors of the domestic economy while continuing to attract foreign investments in the external and domestic sectors of the economy. Deepening the process of economic liberalization could have an additional multiplier effect on the economy: Market reforms could facilitate improved relations with the United States, because they would fulfill one of the criteria for lifting the U.S. embargo specified under the 1992 Cuban Democracy Act.[2]

The problem is that market reforms entail high political and ideological costs for the regime. They undermine the regime's control over society by opening the door to the emergence of a new private sector. They tend to demoralize the regime's cadres in the Party, government, and security forces, who must make do on fixed incomes. They alienate even more poorly paid workers and retirees, who are most dependent on subsidized goods and services. Because the market rewards individual economic initiative, resourcefulness, and enterprise, rather than political loyalty and revolutionary commitment, the reforms also produce new forms of social stratification. The market thus works against the regime's traditional political constituencies and undermines its ideological appeal.

During 1993, for example, Party rank-and-file members and other loyalists complained that the less revolutionary committed—among them, the *jineteros* (hustlers and pimps) and *jineteras* (prostitutes) and others who ply their trade to tourists and earn dollars—were precisely the ones benefiting most from the "dollarization" of the economy in 1993, a move that decriminalized the possession of dollars in order to stabilize the economy. The sharp fall in the value of the *peso* and the cutbacks in subsidized services under the government's austerity program similarly eroded regime support among workers the following year. The expected layoffs of 500,000 or more employees from state enterprises would further weaken popular support.

Hence, while liberalization will speed Cuba economic recovery, the regime will have to find ways to offset the political fallout from new austerity measures and other unpopular policies. In the meantime, the government's hesitant, limited approach to economic reforms reflects this contradiction between the regime's economic and politi-

---

[2]Irrespective of the CDA, the marketization and at least partial privatization of the Cuban economy are needed to break the concentrated economic and political power of the state, thereby creating the economic basis for the emergence and maintenance of political democracy on the island.

cal imperatives, with the result that the economy remained bifurcated and in limbo during 1995.

POLITICAL LIBERALIZATION TO REGAIN LEGITIMACY

Cuba's strong authoritarian system has helped the regime ride out
the 5-year-old economic crisis and maintain political stability. But
its legitimacy and basis of popular support have been shrinking for
political as well as economic reasons. The "nation" no longer con-
sists exclusively of dedicated revolutionaries but must now include
those Cubans—probably a substantial majority—who are politically
alienated, consider the regime illegitimate, and would vote the government out of office if given the opportunity. If popular support
continues to erode, the regime may be able to maintain political
stability by relying on its totalitarian social controls. In time,
however, the political situation would become further polarized and
volatile, making peaceful change less likely.

The regime is counting on the island's economic recovery to relegitimize and maintain itself in power. But political liberalization may
also be required if the leadership is to defuse anti-regime sentiment
and reconstitute the political community in a way that ensures stability and peaceful change. To do so, the regime would have to relinquish the Party's vanguard status and sole claim to power. It would
have to begin an open, give-and-take dialogue with political dissidents and other emerging civil society actors. It would have to allow
open, fair elections in which opposition parties would organize
themselves and compete freely for political power on a level playing
field.

However, such political liberalization remains anathema to Castro
and most of the Cuban leadership. They are mindful of what occurred in the Soviet Union after Gorbachev introduced *glasnost* and
perestroika. Castro advised President Daniel Ortega and the *Sandinistas* not to risk losing power by agreeing to the February 25, 1990,
internationally supervised elections in Nicaragua. Since then, the
Cuban *caudillo* has time and again voiced his contempt for bourgeois democracy while rejecting the counsel of the Spanish and other
friendly governments urging him to liberalize the Cuban polity.

Despite international appeals, Cuba's last round of municipal elections in July 1995 conformed pretty much to past practices: No political parties were permitted to field candidates, including the ruling Communist Party. But the list of 29,000 electoral candidates was carefully screened, and the government insisted on "solidarity" and "unity" from the electorate. The regime was bent on retaining political power and control, even at the municipal level.

In the meantime, pleas for opening up Cuba's political process continued to fall on deaf ears, even when they came from moderate sectors of the Cuban exile community, which the regime had begun to court. The most prominent of these is Eloy Gutíerrez Menoyo, a former guerrilla commander who was sent to prison for 22 years in 1964, after he broke with the regime over the issue of elections and organized a rebellion. Now living in Miami, Gutíerrez Menoyo formed *Cambio Cubano* (Cuban Change), which advocates dialogue with the Castro government as a means of securing Cuba's peaceful transition to democracy.

In June 1995, Gutíerrez Menoyo returned to Cuba and was received by Castro. He asked that *Cambio Cubano* be allowed to participate freely in Cuban politics but was unable to secure a commitment from the Cuban leader. For Castro, on the other hand, meeting his opponent had enabled him to display his flexibility to the world, score points with liberal circles abroad, and sow seeds of open discord within the exile community over the dialogue issue.

That Castro's intent in receiving Gutíerrez Menoyo had nothing to do with advancing the cause of democracy was confirmed by subsequent developments. In November 1995, the Cuban Government convened its second conference on "the nation and emigration," which was attended by some 350 exiles from the United States and elsewhere, among them Gutíerrez Menoyo and other moderate exile leaders, as well as those sympathetic to the regime. At the conference, Gutíerrez Menoyo appealed for the opening up of the Cuban polity and respect for human rights. He used Foreign Minister Roberto Robaina's criticism of the U.S. embargo to remind conference delegates that "there are two embargoes, one American and one Cuban," while calling for a "multi-party scenario" and the rewriting of the Cuban constitution to protect citizens from abuse by the state.[3]

However, except for Foreign Minister Robaina's announcement facilitating travel to the island by the 1.2 million Cubans living abroad, Gutíerrez Menoyo came away empty-handed. Ricardo Alarcón, President of the National Assembly, rejected the appeal for a political opening by asserting that "some people have discussed things from a level totally detached from reality." Alarcón went on to insist that "only Cubans [residing in Cuba] decide in Cuba" the issue of whether there is political change or lack of change.[4]

Buoyed by his public reception in New York on the occasion of his visit to the United Nations, Castro himself made clear that Cuba's democratization was on permanent hold. Interviewed by Telemundo, a Spanish-language TV network in the United States, the Cuban president was adamant in denying dissidents or opposition groups access to the state media: "I will be frank with you. . . . They have no access, and they will have none, because we are not going to give any opportunity to those who want to destroy the revolution."[5]

THE BREADTH AND INTENSITY OF REGIME OPPOSITION

Despite the acute economic crisis, widespread popular discontent, and eroding political legitimacy, the regime has not confronted opposition on any mass scale except for the Havana riots in August 1994. Apart from the effectiveness of the state's security apparatus and the weakness of civil society actors, there are several reasons for Cuba's anemic political opposition.

One reason is that, whether out of conviction, necessity, or lack of feasible alternatives, some sectors of the population either actively support the regime or at least passively accept it. That the economic situation improved a bit during 1995 strengthens this type of supportive behavior. In the July 1995 municipal elections, in which the

---

[3]Larry Rohter, "Havana Moves to Ease the Way for Emigres Who Live in the U.S. to Invest in Cuba," *The New York Times*, November 7, 1995, p. A11.

[4]"ANAP President Discusses Migration," *FBIS-LAT-95-216*, November 8, 1995, p. 4.

[5]Larry Rohter, "A Little Hope," 1995, p. E3.

electorate could vote for the regime's list of approved candidates, only 11.2 percent of the voters invalidated or left blank their ballot as a sign of opposition. In his July 26 speech, Castro hailed this election outcome as a measure of public solidarity with, and confidence in, his government, despite Cuba's hard times.[6]

Race is another factor benefiting the regime. Constituting some 50 percent of the population, blacks and mulattos have been among the regime's most stalwart supporters because, on the whole, they are among the chief socioeconomic beneficiaries of the revolution. Although disproportionately few Afro-Cubans hold top Party and government positions, blacks and mulattos have nevertheless enjoyed striking political and socioeconomic mobility. Some have found a place in the upper ranks of the officer class in the Revolutionary Armed Forces (FAR) and the Ministry of Interior. Others form part of Cuba's educated, professional class of teachers, doctors, scientists, and technicians. Understandably, therefore, many fear the return of the rich, predominantly white exile leadership in Miami, and have cast their lot with the regime.

Anti-regime sentiment remains diffused among the general population, because that population lacks political and intellectual leadership. Human-rights, dissident, and opposition groups have mushroomed in recent years; many of their leaders have displayed extraordinary courage in confronting the regime. Nonetheless, these groups are struggling against terrible odds.

Many are fragmented, in rivalry with one another, and infiltrated by government informers. Opposition leaders are frequently harassed, face short-term detentions by the Ministry of Interior, or are imprisoned for longer terms on charges of sowing "enemy propaganda"

---

[6]An 11-percent invalidation, or annulment, rate might appear to be a relatively high indicator of popular opposition, especially when compared with the 97–99-percent voter approval rates reported by the former Soviet Union and other communist states. In actuality, however, the July 1995 invalidation, or annulment, rate was lower than in the February 1993 municipal elections. The 1993 rate ranged from 20 percent according to the Mexican press, to 15 percent in Havana, to 7 percent outside the capital, according to Agence France Presse. On the background and outcome of the 1993 elections, see Gonzalez and Ronfeldt, *Storm Warnings for Cuba*, 1994, pp. 33–34.

and "disrespect" against the state.[7] Some 600 "prisoners of conscience" are believed to be awaiting trial or are serving prison sentences. Those that are released from prison often gain their freedom only on condition that they leave Cuba permanently.[8]

Independent intellectuals and journalists who dare criticize the regime are similarly subject to harassment and imprisonment. Of the 10 intellectuals who signed the June 1991 "Declaration of Cuban Intellectuals," which, among other things, called for a national debate and direct and free elections, all but two were forced into exile, some after being beaten up and imprisoned.[9]

The director of the recently created Independent Press Bureau of Cuba (BPIC), Indamiro Restano, was released and paroled in June 1995 through the intercession of former French President Francois Mitterand's wife. However, he cannot publish news for internal consumption. "Journalists in Cuba," he said in an October 1995 interview, "have always lived between autocensorship and jail."[10] A few days later, Olance Nogueras Roce was arrested as he left the BPIC office and was placed in a high-security prison, evidently because he had written an article on government plans to complete Cuba's nuclear plant.[11]

Potential opposition leadership is further diminished by the regime's co-optation of much of the intelligentsia. The regime uses the silk glove with those in the intelligentsia who are prepared to conform and not openly criticize the regime. Progovernment journalists, writers, artists, musicians, film directors, academics, and others among the intelligentsia are given better housing and state support for their work, and are allowed to travel and earn income abroad.

---

[7]In April 1995, for example, a military tribunal sentenced human-rights activist Francisco Chivano to 15 years in prison.

[8]Excerpts from the Amnesty International Report 1995, "Cuba," as reprinted in Freedom House, *Cuba Brief*, June 1995, p. 3.

[9]On the declaration and fate of those who signed it, including the poetess María Elena Cruz Varela, see International Republican Institute, *Dissenting Voices*, Vol. 1, No. 2, July 1995, pp. 1–8.

[10]"BPIC Director Indamiro Restano Comments on Cuba, Castro," *FBIS-LAT-95-202*, October 19, 1995, p. 28.

[11]"Group Reports Arrest of Independent Journalist," *FBIS-LAT-95-207*, October 26, 1995, pp. 2–3.

As a result, Cuba thus far is unlike several of the former communist-bloc states of Eastern Europe, especially Poland with its militant Solidarity movement, East Germany with its outspoken Lutheran clergy, and Czechoslovakia with its growing student and intellectual opposition circles. Lacking a strong civil society to channel their demands and grievances, Cubans have thus far engaged in anomic-type spontaneous outbursts against the government, as during the Havana riots of August 1994 and Cojimar's street protests a year earlier.

In the meantime, the vast majority of discontented Cubans remain politically inert for any number of reasons:

- They fear reprisals from state security organs.

- They fear the prospects of social upheaval.

- They fear the return of vengeful right-wing exiles.

- They hope to leave Cuba one way or another.

- They hope that the economic and political situation will improve.

- They hope that Castro and other leaders will embrace peaceful change.

- They hope that the United States will lift the embargo or somehow improve their personal prospects and those of Cuba.

But whatever their personal reasons, most Cubans so far have been unwilling to challenge the regime.

As demonstrated by the current crisis, deteriorating economic and political conditions are in themselves insufficient causes for mass opposition. Cuba's defused, dissipated antigovernment sentiment will itself have to undergo a qualitative, as well as quantitative, transformation if fundamental political and economic change is to be impelled from below. Changes in political perceptions, risk aversion, and personal expectations will be required of individual Cubans for political opposition to grow and become widespread, organized, and active. As signaled by the emergence of *Concilio Cubano* and a revitalized Catholic Church (see also Chapter Five), such a societal transformation has begun, but it may take years before a more assertive civil society emerges.

SECURITY FORCES: AVOIDING A CUBAN TIANANMEN

Thus far, the regime's internal security organs have succeeded in preventing and containing the rise of opposition groups. As a result, the government has avoided confronting a mass-based opposition movement similar to what occurred in China at Tiananmen Square in 1989. Only during the Cojimar protests in July 1993 and, especially, the Havana riots a year later did the regime have to deal with large-scale civil unrest.

Moreover, the regime has shown itself to be adept at learning from its mistakes. There was agreement within the regime that the Party and security forces had committed tactical errors in Cojimar, a town on the outskirts of Havana, where excessive repression was employed to crush the protesters in July 1993. Despite the fact that they were much larger in scale, the Havana riots were handled later with relatively less physical violence, through the judicious deployment of the National Revolutionary Police, the Blas Roca Rapid Reaction Brigade, and special Ministry of Interior units trained in riot control.

As is discussed in Chapter Four, if the economy resumes its downward spiral and unrest spreads, the regime must maintain political control of the streets. If such control is lost, the regime will have no alternative but to call in Army units to restore order. Whether the Army continues loyal to, or divides and turns against, the regime if units are required to fire upon civilian protesters remains to be seen.

REGIME COHESIVENESS

Thus far, the Castro regime has displayed remarkable staying power and cohesiveness, despite the severity of the crisis since the fall of the Soviet Union in 1991. Other than the trial and execution of Division General Arnaldo Ochoa in summer 1989 and a few mid-level civilian and military defections since then, the regime has not been rent by major ruptures within its ranks.

As is discussed in detail in the next chapter, part of the reason for the leadership's internal cohesiveness is the authority exercised by Fidel and Raúl Castro and the loyalty of their trusted *fidelista* and *raulista* lieutenants, who control key organs of power in the Party, military, and security forces. But there are other reasons the regime has not experienced the divisions and unraveling that affected most East European communist regimes at the end of the 1980s.

Despite the appointment of younger leaders to government and Party posts, the Castro regime is unlike its former East European brethren in that it is still led by first-generation revolutionaries and nationalists. Even though many may no longer subscribe to their original utopian goals, these founding members of the Cuban Revolution still have a strong personal and historical stake in the Revolution's final outcome. Many, beginning with Castro himself, may prefer to end their careers as revolutionary martyrs rather than join the ranks of Cuba's failed, corrupt, cynical leaders of the past.[12]

Another reason is that, despite differences in age, education and training, and policy preferences, the leadership has no other alternative but to stand together with Fidel and Raúl. As the East European and Soviet cases demonstrate, divisions within the internal elite could sink the regime. This is particularly true for the Cuban leadership: Not only must it guard against domestic enemies among the island's population, it also fears annihilation from abroad—by exiles in Florida and by the regime's historic enemy, the United States.

For their part, the Castro brothers have been adept in grooming the younger generation for positions of power and influence, particularly in the Party and government. This "greening of the Revolution" began with the Fourth Party Congress in October 1991, when several veteran leaders were replaced in the 25-member Political Bureau by no less than nine new members who were in their thirties and forties. This process of renewal continues today. The latest shake-up of provincial Party secretaries saw three old-guard leaders succeeded by thirty- and forty-year-olds. As a consequence, all 14 of Cuba's

---

[12]On aspects of Castro's political personality that may incline him in this direction, see Edward Gonzalez and David Ronfeldt, *Castro, Cuba, and the World*, Santa Monica, Calif.: RAND, R-3420, June 1986, pp. 3–62. On the broader historical factors of Cuban political culture and revolutionary martyrdom that may affect other leaders as well, see Nelson P. Valdes, "Cuban Political Culture: Between Betrayal and Death," in Sandor Halebsky and John M. Kirk, eds., *Cuba in Transition: Crisis and Transformation*, Boulder, Colo.: Westview Press, 1992, pp. 221–222.

provincial secretaries now range in age from 34 to 47 years. They, in turn, expect to be among the heirs to the aging revolutionary leadership.[13]

Nevertheless, the ultimate test of regime cohesiveness may still lie ahead. If the economy starts to worsen again and public unrest spreads, the loyalty and commitment of some elites could be strained. At the very least, divisions within the leadership are likely to intensify over how best to respond to the worsening crisis. It is to these individual leaders and institutional actors that we now turn.

---

[13]See "New Political Faces," *CubaNews*, August 1995, p. 12.

Chapter Four

REGIME LEADERS, TENDENCIES, AND INSTITUTIONAL PLAYERS

Fidel and, to a lesser degree, his brother, Raúl, remain the regime's undisputed leaders. They retain the personal loyalty and support of their respective followers, the *fidelistas* and *raulistas*, many of whom were guerrilla combatants with the Castro brothers.[1] But the regime is no longer as monolithic or as personalistic as it once was. More than ever before, it has become a more diverse coalition of elites as a result of Cuba's crisis.

Castro has had to turn to a younger generation of civilian and military leaders who possess the technical training, managerial expertise, and other skills needed for Cuba's recovery and continued stability. In turn, the crisis has produced three major policy tendencies within the leadership—alternative political and economic formulas for ensuring regime survival, around which are clustered the *duros*, *centristas*, and *reformistas*. Variously aligned with each of these tendencies are the regime's institutional actors—the Party, the armed forces, and internal security forces—and the new leadership generation composed of so-called Yummies (young, upwardly mobile communists).

How the power and influence among these key regime players remains distributed within the coalition will, in large measure, determine the regime's response to future developments and its choice of policy alternatives. As will be seen in Part II, however, U.S. policy

---

[1]Beginning with the Fourth Party Congress in October 1991, many of these former comrades-in-arms retired from top leadership positions and are now referred to as *históricos* (historic ones).

could affect the standing of individual players and help one or more of the competing policy tendencies to ascend.

THE CASTRO DYNASTY

The Cuban *Caudillo*

The single most important variable determining Cuba's immediate future is whether Fidel Castro, who became 69 years old in August 1995, remains in good health and physically present. The young, charismatic "Fidel," who once inspired his followers with his infallibility and revolutionary conviction, has given way to "Castro," the aging *caudillo* intent on retaining power and ensuring his place in history. Still, he continues as Cuba's towering patriarch and supreme leader, whose presence helps to legitimize the regime and preserve its internal cohesion.

Within the Cuban leadership, Castro's moral authority is not solely derived from his role as the founder of the Cuban Revolution. It also stems from his skill, intelligence, and audacity in successfully defying the United States, catapulting Cuba onto the world stage, and ensuring his regime's survival in critical times, as has been the case since the disappearance of the Soviet Union. As one member of the Political Bureau's new generation of leaders confided to Andres Oppenheimer in the early 1990s, "Fidel has long headlights. He makes mistakes, but fewer than the rest of us. You can't dismiss his political genius."[2]

While Castro knows that his regime must introduce some reforms if it is to survive, his sympathies lie with the *duros*, the hardliners. He remains opposed to fundamental system change, in part for personal reasons—among them, his strong aversion to capitalism, his fear that any dismantling of "Cuban socialism" will tarnish his unique place in history, and his concern that his power will be eroded by economic, as well as political, reforms. He is fully aware that *perestroika* and *glasnost* led to the dissolution of the Soviet Union, and that democratic elections in Nicaragua, which was experiencing a severe eco-

---

[2]Andres Oppenheimer, *Castro's Final Hour—The Story Behind the Coming Downfall of Communist Cuba*, New York: Simon and Schuster, 1992, p. 404.

nomic crisis as well as internal war, led to the ouster of the *Sandinista* government in 1990.

However, the Cuban leader needs neither the Soviet nor the Nicaraguan example to turn him against political liberalization, because he has never been one to soften, much less relinquish, his regime's control mechanisms over society. At a 1987 meeting of the Political Bureau, well before the onset of the current crisis, he vehemently rejected suggestions from Raúl, Division General Abelardo Colomé, and others to provide a safety valve for political dissent. He reminded them that they had initially been alone at the outset of the anti-Batista struggle and that, if needed, his regime would now rule as a "minority government." He warned against any softening toward "social indiscipline" or political dissent, adding that he would unleash "revolutionary terror" in the streets against any manifestation of popular opposition.[3] Thus were born the Rapid Reaction Brigades, goon squads composed of club-wielding workers that are used by the Ministry of Interior to beat up dissidents, human-rights activists, and antigovernment protesters.

Early on in the current transition process, many Cubans inside and outside the regime hoped that Castro would lead and legitimize the economic and political reforms that Cuba required. For some of the regime's reformers, however, *cambio con Fidel* ("change with Fidel") has now become an oxymoron because of his stubborn resistance to system change.

In his July 26, 1995, speech, Castro made clear his opposition to the market system, or what he prefers to call "capitalism," which he blamed for causing the destruction of the Soviet Union. In contrast, China and Vietnam were showing how some "quite radical" (market-type) measures could be introduced to make Cuba's economy more efficient and adaptive to the realities of today's world. But Cuba would not embark upon "a return to capitalism, or much worse, an insane and hysterical race in that direction." Indeed, he criticized

---

[3]Interview with Jésus Renzoli, former Second Chief of the Second Secretary of the PCC, 1983–1990, and former Chief of the Cuban Military Mission to the Soviet Union, 1990–1992, in Washington, D.C., June 9, 1994. As Raúl Castro's assistant, Renzoli transcribed the minutes of the Political Bureau meetings for him.

the pernicious effects that Cuba's modest reforms had already had on society's moral fiber:

> Examples of corruption and blackmail, which we never witnessed during 30 years of trade with the USSR, are gradually taking place and growing in our economic relations with capitalism. The struggle that the party and government will have to undertake against these trends before they turn into a cancer that devours our ethics and revolutionary spirit will have to be a colossal one. The blood of so many [martyrs] was not spilled for nothing to allow such a pathetic conduct in this most difficult hour of the fatherland.[4]

For the time being, those leadership circles who want change are unwilling to take on Cuba's socialist *caudillo*. Instead, many are looking to Raúl as their best hope for promoting still more economic reforms.

The Growing Prominence of Raúl Castro

Bound by blood ties and the guerrilla struggle, Raúl has been his brother's most trusted lieutenant, as well as designated heir to the revolutionary throne. He is second only to Fidel in controlling the helm of power. As General of the Army and Minister of the Revolutionary Armed Forces, he has controlled the military since 1959. He is Second-Secretary of the Communist Party of Cuba, and first in line after his brother to head the state and government of Cuba. Now, having turned 64 years of age in June 1995, he is emerging as the principal force behind Cuba's modest reform efforts.

Raúl remains a committed communist and a *fidelista*, but he has always been far more pragmatic and administratively competent than his older brother. Learning from the failure of the East European communist states, especially Poland, he early on saw the need for reforming aspects of Cuban socialism to avoid communism's fate elsewhere. Starting in the mid-1980s, he quietly began to improve military enterprises by introducing greater managerial and worker discipline and by adopting Western and Japanese managerial techniques. By no means a free-marketeer, he nevertheless saw the need

---

[4]"Fidel Castro Speaks," 1995, p. 7.

to employ market mechanisms and practices to improve productivity.

Thus, Raúl, the Army, and a younger generation of civilian leaders and technocrats, many personally linked to him, are spearheading the economic changes that the regime has so far implemented. Obtaining Castro's grudging go-ahead and that of other hardliners, they have pressed forward with limited, incremental reforms to stabilize the economy and prevent a political crisis. Thus, in September 1994, Raúl announced the long-awaited reopening and enlargement of the farmers' markets—a measure that for years had been vetoed by his brother, but whose time had now come after the Havana riots the previous month.

On the other hand, Raúl is every bit as uncompromising as his brother when it comes to internal security and the United States. In November 1995, on the thirty-third anniversary of the founding of Military Counterintelligence, he lashed out at the Cuban Democracy Act for combining "openly hostile" means (i.e., tightening the embargo under Track I of the CDA) with "supposedly peaceful ties" (increased telecommunication and people-to-people contacts under CDA's Track II) in order to overthrow the regime and "impose a made-in-Washington model." He warned of U.S. attempts at personal communications with, and special treatment of, the Revolutionary Armed Forces and the Ministry of Interior, which had "the intent of ideologically undermining us from inside." As an antidote, he called for strengthening the role of the Communist Party "as a leading and cohesive vanguard of all patriotic forces," and for increased vigilance by state security organizations.[5]

POLICY TENDENCIES WITHIN THE REGIME

Since 1989, three policy tendencies have emerged within the leadership: *duros*, *centristas*, and *reformistas*. All three share a strong consensus on retaining exclusive power for the present leadership, on the imperative of protecting Cuba's sovereignty and independence from U.S. encroachments, and on the need to preserve some form of social safety net for the populace. But they differ over the degree of

---

[5]"Raúl Castro Discusses Talks with U.S.," *FBIS-LAT-95-223*, November 20, 1995, p. 8.

economic and, to a lesser extent, political liberalization needed to ride out Cuba's current crisis. These leadership differences over policy alternatives account for the erratic, stop-and-start nature of the reform process in recent years.[6]

The *Duros*

The hardliners, or *duros,* represent the dominant tendency—or at least the one possessing veto power over policy—if only because they resonate with and, at times, are led by Fidel Castro. Many of the old veteran revolutionaries, older provincial Party leaders, and Ministry of Interior personnel can be found among their ranks in the Political Bureau and other high-level organs. Besides Fidel, the *duros* include Political Bureau members José Ramón Machado Ventura, Esteban Lazo, Provincial First Secretary Jorge Lezcano, and Division General Abelardo Colomé of the Ministry of Interior. As committed *fidelista* communists, the *duros* adamantly oppose concessions to Washington and, with Fidel in the lead, are prepared to use force to quash opposition to the regime. They also oppose any form of economic liberalization that would lead to a loss of state control over society and would allow the reemergence of a large private sector and bourgeoisie. They thus serve as a brake on the implementation of economic and political reforms.

The *Centristas*

The second, increasingly influential, tendency is represented by the centrists, led by Raúl Castro, Economy and Planning Minister José Luis Rodríguez,[7] and the military as an institution. Their ranks include National Assembly President Ricardo Alarcón, some of the younger Political Bureau members (such as Abel Prieto), and Division Generals Ulises Rosales del Toro and Julio Casas Rigueiro. The influence of the *centristas* has grown in recent years because they offer technical solutions and market-type mechanisms for cop-

---

[6]A full elaboration of the three tendencies can be found in Gonzalez and Ronfeldt, *Storm Warnings for Cuba,* 1994, pp. 13–28.

[7]José Luis Rodríguez initially served as Finance Minister; in May 1995, he was promoted to his new ministerial post and to Vice President in the Council of Ministers.

ing with the economic crisis without advocating the adoption of a market-driven system.

As committed communists, the *centristas* generally share a common stance with the hardliners on most political and security issues. But they differ from the *duros* in that they are ready to adopt some liberalizing reforms that would help preserve the essential features of Cuban socialism, including its state-directed economy and social safety net, which includes free health care and education, and unemployment and retirement benefits. They thus advocate adopting market-type mechanisms and Western- or Japanese-type managerial techniques to overcome consumer-goods shortages, make state enterprises more efficient, and reduce the government's deficit.

In September 1994, for example, it was Raúl who announced the reopening and enlargement of the farmers' markets and the creation of similar markets for crafts and surplus state goods. Economy and Planning Minister Rodríguez has also taken the lead in arguing for reduced state expenditures and greater fiscal discipline. He has called for cutbacks in subsidies to state enterprises and for laying off unneeded workers in the public sector.

The *Reformistas*

Unlike the centristas, the regime's genuine reformers are inclined to move more rapidly toward a market economy—a position that, in large measure, weakens them as a policy tendency. The ranks of the *reformistas* are filled predominantly by the new generation of regime leaders.

At the top, the reformists have included Carlos Lage, a Political Bureau member who serves as the architect for economic reforms in his capacity as Vice President in the Council of State. Lately, however, Lage has become a less-visible, less-assertive *reformista*; he may well have crossed over to the *centrista* camp.

Other *reformista* officials include Foreign Minister Roberto Robaina and, until his May 12 removal, Economy and Planning Minister

Osvaldo Martínez.[8] Francisco Soberón, who was appointed President of the National Bank in January 1995, appears to be a rising star among the *reformistas*, as evidenced by his bold steps to reorganize and expand the authority of the National Bank along Western lines.[9] Other lower-level reformers, such as Julio Carranza and Pedro Monreal, staff research centers and economic, technical, and scientific agencies in the government. Because it does not control the helm of the ship of state, however, this latter group has little direct influence over policy.

The *reformistas* want the regime to ease up politically along the lines of Gorbachev's *glasnost*, to allow some political space for a loyal opposition, without, however, the regime conceding power. On the economic side, they not only advocate foreign investments, Cuba's rapid insertion into the world economy, and the employment of market mechanisms. They also appear ready to embrace a market system for a mixed economy—one that would include a large, Cuban-owned private sector, as well as state and cooperative sectors—as the only way to revitalize the economy.

For the most part, the *reformistas* have only partially succeeded in advancing their agenda. Because of the socialist convictions of Castro and the *duros*, they have had to take care in how they formulate and justify their reform proposals so that they are not accused of returning Cuba to its discredited capitalist past. Their success has usually come by being in alliance with Raúl and the *centristas*, and then only when the worsening state of the economy, rising popular discontent, and/or foreign-investor needs have made it imperative for the regime to adopt reforms. Such a conjunction occurred in July 1993 with the dollarization of the economy. It occurred with the

---

[8]Martínez served less than five months as Minister of Economy and Planning. Although his removal was apparently due to poor health, his departure was viewed by many foreign observers as a blow to the reform process, which once again appears to be stalled. *CubaNews*, June 1995, p. 3.

[9]Prior to heading the National Bank, Soberón had had several years of overseas experience in international finance and shipping. His reforms include steps to make the National Bank responsible for issuing currency and maintaining its stability; proposing and implementing monetary policy; supervising the entire banking system; seeking external financing for the economy; and compiling accurate national accounts data, using the methodology recommended by the International Monetary Fund. See "Bank Overhaul Planned," *CubaNews*, December 1995, p. 2.

reintroduction of the farmers' markets after the Havana riots and immigration crisis of August and September 1994. And it may have occurred again with the latest bank reforms, which were prompted by the realization that a "new look" economy and banking system were urgently needed to provide a modern financial infrastructure for Western investors.

INSTITUTIONAL ACTORS AND THE YUMMIES

Crisscrossing these three policy tendencies are the regime's major institutional actors—the Communist Party, the Revolutionary Armed Forces, and the Ministry of Interior—and the newly emerging Yummies, who occupy posts not only inside but also outside the Party and government.[10] These actors may promote or retard economic reforms according to how reforms advance their institutional and personal self-interests, or, at the very least, they tend to view specific reforms through a particular institutional lens.

The Communist Party

Conceived and organized as a Leninist vanguard party, with a membership of over 600,000, the PCC remains Cuba's "sovereign institution." It thus controls major government and state organs, including the armed forces, through its Party membership and network of cadres.

Although it still wields uncontested power, the Party has been weakened by the collapse of communism worldwide. It no longer can legitimize itself through its identification with a universal, historical force. Having lost its ideological lodestar, the Party's authority has been further eroded by the severe economic crisis that Cubans have had to endure over the past five years.

Hence, it is in the Party's interest to promote the island's rapid recovery, lest it find itself shorn of popular support and any vestiges of political legitimacy. The problem is that economic liberalization

---

[10]As far as this author can determine, Andres Oppenheimer, in his book *Castro's Final Hour* (1992), was the first to employ the word *Yummies* to describe the new generation of communists.

threatens the Party's political power and societal control. Market reforms also undermine the morale of PCC cadres, who, for the most part, must live on fixed government incomes and are thus disadvantaged in both relative and absolute terms by an economy that does not reward political loyalty.

As an institution, therefore, the Party tends to be a conservative force whose leadership and cadres resonate more with the sentiments of the *duros* or *centristas* than with those of the *reformistas*. It is, after all, a Leninist party concerned with power and ideology—not with market reforms that would negate its very essence as a political organization. Hence, the PCC may find itself relegated more and more to the political sphere if its economic role becomes less relevant. It stands in contrast to the military, which has assumed an increasingly important economic mission in Cuba's transition process.

The Revolutionary Armed Forces

As the heir to Castro's Rebel Army, which overthrew Batista, and as a founding revolutionary institution created in 1959, the Revolutionary Armed Forces enjoys an intrinsic legitimacy that eludes the PCC. In succeeding decades since 1959, the FAR's legitimacy has been renewed through its defense of the fatherland, its successful overseas combat missions in Africa, and its identification as a "people's army." Starting in 1989, the FAR's institutional clout was further strengthened because high-ranking Army officers were given control of the Ministry of Interior following the latter's large-scale purge.

Since then, the disappearance of Cuba's Soviet patron and the economic crisis that followed, and the consequent severe cutbacks in defense expenditures, have taken their toll on the FAR's military capabilities.[11] In 1990, the total number of active-duty personnel in the FAR stood at 180,000, then declined by less than 7,000 to 173,500 as of 1993. After 1993, however, the FAR was downsized far more drastically: The number of active-duty personnel dropped to 105,000 in 1995 or, according to Defense Intelligence Agency estimates, to an

---

[11]Except where otherwise noted, the following information is based on Phyllis Greene Walker's "Cuba's Revolutionary Armed Forces: Adapting in the New Environment," *Cuban Studies, Estudios Cubanos*, Vol. 96, forthcoming in January 1997.

even lower figure of 60,000 to 80,000.[12] The Army accounts for over 80 percent of either figure; for all practical purposes, it has been reduced to an infantry force, because some 75 percent of major ground equipment is now in storage. The Air Force and Navy have had much of their equipment retired or cannibalized for parts. The acute shortage of fuel has further reduced the combat readiness of the Air Force.[13]

Such a sharp decline in personnel and military capabilities could put a strain on the FAR's loyalty to and support for the regime, particularly in view of the Cuban military's self-image and reputation as a first-class fighting force. However, three offsetting factors have helped keep the FAR in line during Cuba's acute economic and political crisis:[14] personal, professional, and Party ties; a new mission; and a crisis role.

Personal, Professional, and Party Ties. The Castro brothers have ensured the military's loyalty in typical Latin American fashion, by maintaining personal bonds between themselves and the FAR's senior officers, many of whom fought with Fidel and Raúl against Batista. But Soviet training, the heightened sense of professionalism and *esprit de corp*s instilled by the successful African expeditions, and the high rate of Communist Party membership among officers (88 percent) have also helped to distinguish the FAR from their Latin American brethren. Despite the island's current crisis, the Cuban military remains subordinated and loyal to civilian rule—specifically, to Fidel Castro in his role as Commander in Chief, First Party

---

[12]The DIA estimate was given by Lt. General James R. Clapper, Jr., Director, Defense Intelligence Agency. See U.S. Congress, Senate, Select Committee on Intelligence, *Worldwide Intelligence Review, Hearing Before the Select Committee on Intelligence,* 104th Congress, 1st Session, 1995, p. 168. Walker's figure of 105,000 is based on data in the International Institute for Strategic Studies, *The Military Balance: 1995/1996,* London: Brassey's Inc., 1995, p. 213.

[13]*Worldwide Intelligence Review,* 1995, p. 168. Besides Walker, see also Hal Klepak, "Cuban Security—Old Myths and New Realities," *Jane's Intelligence Review,* Vol. 7, No. 7, July 1995, pp. 334–335.

[14]On the role of the Cuban military in the 1990s, see Richard L. Millett, *Cuba's Armed Forces: From Triumph to Survival,* Washington, D.C.: Georgetown University, Cuba Briefing Paper Series, No. 4, September 1993; A. B. Montes, *The Military Response to Cuba's Economic Crisis,* Washington, D.C.: Defense Intelligence Agency, August 1993; and International Research 2000, Inc., *The Military and Transition in Cuba,* March 17, 1995.

Secretary, and head of state and government, and to Raúl Castro as Minister of the Revolutionary Armed Forces and as second-in-line to Fidel as civilian head of the Party, state, and government.

The military has shown no sign of breaking ranks, even when the reputation and life of one its most prestigious officers was at stake. All the FAR's senior officers stood by the Castro brothers in the 1989 show trial of Division General Arnaldo Ochoa, Cuba's most popular field general, who was accused of money-laundering and other misdeeds. Ochoa's real crime, however, may have been only that he had behaved too independently of the Castro brothers. For that reason, he was feared to be a potential lightning rod for dissent within the officer ranks. His execution, together with that of three other officers from the FAR and the Ministry of Interior, stood as a warning to military men of the fate that would await them if they ever crossed Fidel or Raúl.

The FAR's New Mission. The decline in the FAR's military capabilities has been offset by the Army's new economic mission, which Raúl Castro has promoted since the late 1980s. The military's new mission has strengthened its institutional influence within the regime and, probably, its popular legitimacy.

After improving the productivity of its Military Industrial Enterprises (EMIs) as ordered by Raúl, the Army began to apply its managerial expertise to civilian enterprises, starting in the late 1980s. In recent years, the Army has been in the forefront of the *centristas'* efforts to make the state sector of the economy both more efficient and more productive and to introduce some modest liberalizing measures that would help ease consumer austerity. Together with the Youth Labor Army, which it commands, the Army is growing crops for troop and civilian consumption and is administering military and civilian enterprises. It also runs a number of tourist facilities and activities through its far-flung Gaviota enterprise. It is promoting the adoption of Western-style managerial techniques and market mechanisms in the state sector of the civilian economy.

Although it employs Western managerial techniques and market mechanisms, the FAR probably is opposed to adopting a full-fledged market system. The military has benefited from Cuba's state-controlled economy through not only the EMIs but also the joint enterprises managed by former or active-duty officers. Most officers may also fear that a market economy would undo the Revolution's social gains in such areas as free public health and education and greater socioeconomic equality, and return Cuba to the pre-1959 capitalist order.

In addition to Raúl, such top military leaders as Division Generals Ulises Rosales del Toro (Chief of the General Staff and First Vice-Minister of the MINFAR), Division General Julio Casas Regueiro (Vice-Minister responsible for economic affairs), and his brother, Division General Senen Casas Regueiro (Minister of Transportation), appear to be solidly behind the FAR's new economic mission.[15] Also, a select number of lower- and mid-ranking officers with managerial and business skills can expect to gain from the Army's growing economic role. On the other hand, most line officers may be concerned about the decline in promotional opportunities resulting from the loss of the FAR's military capabilities and internationalist missions.

The FAR's Crisis Role. Cuba's current crisis has made the FAR essential to the regime's survival. That the island has remained in a controlled-crisis mode is due in large part to the continued institutional loyalty to and support of the regime by the military.

Still, the loyalty of the FAR remains to be tested in worst-case situations, situations in which Cuba is enveloped in internal unrest. The armed forces consider themselves the defenders of the Cuban nation and, as a "people's army" recruited from the populace, they are not immune to the suffering of their relatives and friends in the civilian population. Will the officer ranks thus hold if the economy once more suffers a sharp reversal? Will the Army continue to support the regime if Castro and the Party appear less and less capable of ruling effectively? If control of the streets is lost and Army units are called in to deal with civilian rioters and opposition groups, will those units fire on civilian men, women, and children?

---

[15]In *Storm Warnings for Cuba*, the author placed General del Toro and most other senior officers in the hardline camp. Since that study's publication in 1994, however, new information on the FAR, including information from defectors, suggests that most senior officers should be classified as *centristas*, along with Raúl Castro.

The Castro leadership is keenly aware that, to avoid a Tiananmen Square–like confrontation with the civilian populace, it must prevent such extreme contingencies from occurring. Thus, its first line of defense is to deploy the riot-control police, Rapid Reaction Brigades, and, if necessary, the elite Special Troops from the Ministry of Interior. This strategy prevented the Havana riots of August 5, 1994, from spreading, but it might not work again if the economy were to deteriorate anew and popular unrest were to spill onto the streets.

The Ministry of Interior

Despite its shake-up in 1989, the Ministry of Interior remains the regime's first line of defense against internal subversion and opposition. The MININT is also responsible for running foreign intelligence operations under the General Directorate of Intelligence (DGI).

The MININT maintains internal order through its Department of State Security and the General Directorate of Counter-Intelligence (DGCI), which controls a network of spies and informants and has close ties to the neighborhood Committees for the Defense of the Revolution (CDRs). The internal state security apparatus includes the National Revolutionary Police for general police work; the National Special Police Brigade for preventing and handling boat seizures; the Border Guard Troops for guarding the coastline and preventing unauthorized departures; the Rapid Reaction Brigades, which harass dissidents and may be called in to beat up rioters; and the elite Special Troops, which have been trained for riot-control operations.[16]   Tutored by the KGB and East German intelligence, the MININT has over the decades proven itself to be an effective and much-feared security organ.

The MININT's internal security mission places it in a unique relationship to society. Whereas the FAR sees itself as the defender of the *nation* against foreign aggression and identifies itself with the common people, the MININT sees itself as the foremost bastion of the

---

[16]Composed of two battalions numbering some 1,200 men, the elite Special Troops carried out special missions in Angola in 1975.

regime.[17] As a consequence, the MININT always exercises vigilance toward the populace at large and suspects the less revolutionary committed. It wages war against dissidents, human-rights activists, and political opponents, who are seen as internal enemies that threaten the regime's security.

The MININT's security mission necessarily places Army Corps General Abelardo Colomé, the Minister of MININT since 1989, along with most other MININT officers, in the camp of the regime's hard-liners. Of course, many may support the modest reforms advocated by Raúl and the *centristas,* because such measures would not upset society's subordination to the state, and the reforms could make internal security more manageable by correcting some of the sources of popular discontent.

Ultimately, however, the MININT is institutionally among the hard-liners. Its members, more than any other group, would have the most to lose were the regime to collapse or be overthrown: Personal vendettas and legal reprisals against them and their families would be a certainty. Bound to the regime by its mission, the MININT thus will take whatever forceful measures are necessary to ensure regime survival.

The Yummies

The so-called Yummies are the new generation of political leaders, technocrats, managers, expediters, and deal-makers. They have begun to come into their own as a result of Cuba's economic crisis.[18] Some occupy traditional positions of power and influence in the PCC—Lage, Robaina, and Abel Prieto are members of the Political Bureau—or have been newly appointed as most of the Provincial First Secretaries. Others hold positions in the government, state-chartered joint enterprises, and state-sponsored research centers, or

---

[17]As opposed to the *nation,* which is permanently identified with the territory and population of Cuba, *regime* refers to the entire set of government, state, and Party institutions, and the economic system, authoritarian socialist ideology, formal laws, and political processes, etc., that have evolved in Cuba since Castro's assumption of power in 1959.

[18]On the role of the Yummies, see Andres Oppenheimer, *Castro's Final Hour,* 1992, pp. 403ff.

they are freelance business expediters or purchasing agents licensed by the Ministry of Interior and other state agencies.

As communists, the Yummies may be members of the PCC out of conviction or necessity. Some may be full-time Party professionals, but most probably do not consider the Party as their career or as their basis of institutionalized support. Rather, their influence and upward mobility arise from their specialized knowledge as technocrats and from their managerial, entrepreneurial, and marketing skills, which are all needed in a Cuba undergoing economic transition under market-Leninism.

The Yummies thus constitute an amorphous, diffuse lot of individuals. They share the assumption not only that Cuba's economy must transform itself if the regime is to survive but also that their own advancement is directly tied to the success of that transformation. Yet the Yummies are not in agreement on whether Cuba should adopt a market-based economy that rests on domestic and foreign private enterprises or should retain a state-driven economy in which the domestic private sector remains tightly restricted and the state or public sector, along with foreign capital, continues to be dominant.

Thus, some of the Yummies—Lage in the past, and Robaina, Soberón, Carranza, and Monreal today—are among the leading *reformistas* in the regime. But others align themselves with Raúl and the *centristas*, particularly the new civilian and military managers who are administering the joint enterprises, state firms, and production units recently created by the state and MINFAR. Also aligned with the latter may be the new class of brokers and expediters who arrange deals with foreign investors and facilitate economic transactions between foreign capitalist enclaves and the state-run economy.

But whatever their differences, the Yummies see themselves as the rightful heirs of the older generation of revolutionary leaders. Like those leaders, they are not inclined to share power with the regime's opponents. Still, many appear less dogmatic regarding political dissent than Castro and other leaders of the older generation. Hence, as a group, the Yummies may be prepared to permit the existence of a loyal political opposition—but one that would be essentially powerless and whose existence would help dissipate domestic dissent and international criticism of Cuba's authoritarianism. Their relatively greater tolerance may perhaps help pave the way for the emergence of a true civil society in Cuba.

Chapter Five

CIVIL SOCIETY ACTORS

As independent, organized intermediaries, civil society actors played important roles in the demise of communist regimes in several Eastern European countries in 1989—particularly in Poland, where first the Catholic Church and then Solidarity competed with and successfully challenged the power of the Communist state during the 1980s. To a lesser degree, such civil society actors as students, intellectuals, workers, and churches also helped to undermine the rule of communist regimes in Czechoslovakia, Hungary, and East Germany.

Cuba lags these former East European communist countries in the development of a civil society that "lies beyond the boundaries of the family and the clan and beyond the locality," but also "lies short of the state."[1] Fragmented and weak before 1959, Cuban society was afterwards decimated by decades of revolutionary rule, totalitarian social controls, and out-migration. Indeed, the exodus of over 870,000 Cubans to the United States between 1959 and 1994, amounting to nearly 13 percent of the 1959 population, left the island bereft of potential civil society actors—among them, businessmen, professionals, trade unionists, political leaders, students, and clerics. Given conditions of tolerance and civility, they might have formed the basis of a robust civil society.

Nevertheless, there are signs of a nascent civil society in Cuba. The collapse of international communism and the severe economic crisis that ensued on the island weakened the state's grip on society as in-

---

[1]Edward Shils, "The Virtue of Civil Society," *Government and Opposition*, Winter 1991, p. 3.

dividuals increasingly were forced to fend for themselves to survive, relying on the informal economy, or black market, and seeking a livelihood outside the public sector. The erosion of state control over individual behavior, of course, does not make for a civil society. Still, there is now more space between the state and individual Cubans within which independent groups or intermediaries—including nongovernmental organizations (NGOs)—are beginning to arise and function independently of, and even contrary to, the state.

THE CATHOLIC CHURCH

The Catholic Church stands out as the single most important civil society actor in today's Cuba: Not only is it independent of the state, it has also begun to challenge, with considerable care and skill, some of the regime's policies. In a nation that is predominantly Catholic, although not fervently so, the Church possesses a wide following not found with most other civil society actors.

Until recently, the Church was not a strong national institution. Before the Revolution, it had been weakened by its long history of identification with Spain before and after Cuban independence, its narrow middle- and upper-class following, and its inability to attract parishioners among an increasingly secularized and Americanized population. Pummeled by the triumphant Castro regime after 1959, the Church was forced to repatriate its Spanish priests and nuns and to confine itself exclusively to its religious mission. Although the Vatican succeeded in working out a modus vivendi with Castro starting in the late 1960s, the Church remained a submissive institution.

However, the Catholic Church began to recover by the 1980s. The failure of the Revolution to improve substantially the lot of Cuban society after more than three decades and the hardships, regimentation, and grayness imposed by the Castro regime created a spiritual void that the Church began to fill. Recognizing this, Castro took a new, more accommodating approach to religion in the mid-1980s in an effort to bring "believers" back into the revolutionary fold and to play the Protestant churches and Afro-Cuban cults off against the Catholic Church.

But the Castro government was to suffer an unexpected blow. The fall of communism in Eastern Europe and the disappearance of the Soviet Union, which Castro likened to "the sun not rising," eliminated Marxism-Leninism as a secular religion. Whereas Cuba's Communist Party had expected that its more-tolerant policy would attract religious believers to the PCC, it now began to lose some of its old Party members to various religions.

As a result, the Catholic Church has now experienced a remarkable resurgence of its popularity and influence. Not only the old but also the young have begun to attend religious services in growing numbers, with about 250 priests ministering to the population.[2] The Catholic Church's European-based relief agency, Caritas, has established itself as one of the few genuine NGOs operating in Cuba. It has been able to bargain effectively with the Castro government regarding the distribution of medicines and other relief shipments from abroad.[3] Caritas now has seven offices on the island.

The Church hierarchy has also ventured into the political arena. It issued a pastoral letter in September 1993 that criticized Castro for retaining his monopoly on power and called for a dialogue between the regime and its critics. Individual priests have begun to use the pulpit to censure the government for its repressive and divisive policies. And in December 1994, Pope John Paul II elevated Archbishop Jaime Ortega to cardinal, pointedly noting that some of the new cardinals he was appointing had "to endure the oppression of an atheistic, totalitarian regime."[4]

Revitalized as a national institution, the Catholic Church has thus emerged as a singularly influential actor in Cuba's otherwise weak civil society. It possesses the organization, popular constituency, and external support system that could enable it to become a coun-

---

[2]According to one source, attendance at Sunday services is estimated to be about 250,000 for the entire island, about equally divided between Catholics and Protestants. Enrique López Oliva, "Stirrings in Cuba: Religious Reawakening," *Christian Century*, October 1994, pp. 940–941.

[3]See Gillian Gunn, *Cuba's NGOs: Government Puppets or Seeds of Civil Society?* Washington, D.C.: Georgetown University, Cuba Briefing Paper Series, No. 7, February 1995, pp. 5–6.

[4]*CubaInfo*, Vol. 6, No. 16, December 15, 1994, p. 11.

terweight to Cuba's strong state. No longer isolated at home or abroad, the Church has thus ceased to restrict itself solely to its religious mission but, instead, has begun working at the grass-roots level to repair and alter the political consciousness of Cubans.

In the westernmost province of Pinar del Rio, for example, a lay worker has been conducting a 10-week home-study program that already has trained over 1,100 people in the fundamentals of democracy. Attracting small study groups of workers, students, and peasants, the program instills in them a greater sense of self-confidence, initiative, and control over their lives.[5]

However, the Catholic Church has been ever mindful of its institutional interests. Historically, whether in Cuba or elsewhere, it generally has avoided a direct confrontation with tyranny. Thus, it remains to be seen whether Cuba's Catholic Church will flex its political muscles to the point of trying to change government policy or, more boldly still, will openly challenge the regime.

PROTESTANT CHURCHES AND AFRO-CUBAN RELIGIONS

Although they have a weaker institutional structure and international support system than the Catholic Church, other religions have experienced a similar growth in popularity and membership. This is true not only for the Afro-Cuban cults but also for the Christian churches.

Protestant churches, especially the evangelical ones, are attracting a growing following among Afro-Cubans, the young, and the poor. On a 1994 visit to the island, a professor of theology at Drew University was moved by "the emotion and tenacity of a people whose faith could not be extinguished." On a Sunday, he found an Afro-Caribbean Methodist Church on the outskirts of Havana to be "crammed full; no seats anywhere," and "with people of all ages." "It

---

[5]"What are the differences between a mirror, a dog, a prisoner and a man?" the lay worker asks. "Unlike the others, 'a man has intelligence, initiative, creativity and is free. In the 35 years [of Communism], people have lost confidence that they can control their own lives—we're telling them they can.'" Robbins, "Civic Lessons," *The Wall Street Journal*, June 19, 1995, p. 1.

is the Cuban youth," he reports, "who are busy leading their people in religious revival."[6]

An even greater role in this revival has been played by Afro-Cuban religions, which have been deeply ingrained in Cuban society since the eighteenth century, when African slaves openly began to practice them. The three major cults—Santería, Palo Monte, and the Abakua secret societies—were never extinguished by the Revolution—even during its most militant antireligious phase in the 1960s. Unable to stamp them out, the regime struck a truce with the cults that lasted through the 1980s, whereby cult members were allowed to practice their beliefs in private.

Cuba's dispatch of combat soldiers to Angola in the late 1970s and early 1980s led to heightened interest in the Afro-Cuban religions, especially among black and mulatto personnel. After 1989, the hard times that befell Cuba caused an enormous mushrooming of the cults, including within the white population. According to Andres Oppenheimer, this was especially true of the Santería religion, because, unlike with the Catholic Church, Babalao priests offered their worshippers quick comfort and practical relief from life's daily ordeals.[7]

Starting in late 1990, Oppenheimer reports, the Party's Central Committee moved to co-opt the Santeros and the other two Afro-Cuban religions. It had three goals in mind: prevent the cults from being transformed into a political opposition; strengthen grass-roots support for the regime among blacks and the poor; and weaken the Catholic Church, which offered the greatest institutional and doctrinal threat of all the religions. Toward these ends, the Party's Religious Affairs Department greatly increased its political and economic support for Afro-Cuban religious priests; the MININT stepped

---

[6]Thomas C. Oden, "The Church Castro Couldn't Kill," *Christianity Today*, April 25, 1994, p. 19.

[7]"The Santería priests offered quick relief without moralizing sermons. Unlike those of their counterparts in the Catholic Church, their recommendations for physical or spiritual ailments were eminently practical—there was always a concoction to help you fight illness, a prescribed ritual to correct a problem. No matter that you had cheated on your wife, drunk too much or stolen goods from your workplace. The Babalaos were not too interested in the moral issues." Oppenheimer, *Castro's Final Hour*, 1992, p. 341.

up its penetration of the cults; and the media, academic departments, and museums mounted a widespread public-relations campaign that highlighted Santería and progovernment Babalaos.[8]

Even as the basis for a civil society appeared to be emerging with the phenomenal growth of the Afro-Cuban religions, the regime was thus compromising and corrupting these actors to the extent that some were converted into sources of support for the government. As with some of the Protestant churches, the Afro-Cuban cults were more susceptible to state manipulation and penetration than the Catholic Church: Both religions tend to be organized around either individual Protestant ministers or Babalaos; both are bereft of strong, centuries-old institutionalized international support; and both lack the hierarchical structure and cohesive religious doctrine to withstand the machinations of the Cuban state.

According to Oppenheimer, the Communist Party and MININT's Department III-4, which is in charge of religious affairs, were well aware of this vulnerability and sought to turn it to the regime's advantage. After successfully penetrating the Protestant churches, Department III-4 infiltrated the Santería cults with the objective of obtaining political intelligence:

> Nobody knew people's secrets better than Babalaos. . . . If there was an anti-government conspiracy in the making, or if dissidents had recruited large numbers of supporters in a certain part of town, chances were that the Babalaos would hear it soon from relatives or friends worried about the fates of their loved ones.[9]

Government vigilance toward religious groups has not eased since Oppenheimer's account. In June 1995, Amnesty International reported the arrest and sentencing to an 18-month prison term of a Pentecostal minister in Camaguey. He had refused the order of state security agents to stop using his home as a religious meeting place. At his summary trial, 1,000 people reportedly stood outside the court shouting, "Long live Christ." In the meantime, the government had

---

[8]Oppenheimer, 1992, pp. 342–355.

[9]Oppenheimer, 1992, p. 352.

closed down 85 of the 101 evangelical centers in Camaguey, leaving open only the poorest and least-accessible congregations.[10]

SECULAR NONGOVERNMENTAL ORGANIZATIONS

Whereas many religious groups have been carefully watched, penetrated, and, in some cases, closed down by the state, the state permitted—to use Gillian Gunn's words—an "explosive growth" in nongovernment organizations after 1989. She reports that approximately 2,200 so-called NGOs, including religious ones, were registered with the government by the end of 1994.[11]

As Gunn points out, the growth in NGOs was not due to the government's sudden conversion to the virtues of pluralism but to sheer economic necessity. What she is less clear about is whether the vast majority of these NGOs are, in fact, *nongovernmental* in the true sense of the term—that is, organizations that are ideologically, politically, and financially independent of the state.

With the loss of Soviet subsidies, the Castro government was obliged to look elsewhere for external sources of funding. Starting in 1990, the government allowed Cuban NGOs—many of which had formerly been front organizations or otherwise financially dependent upon the state—to tap foreign NGOs for financial assistance. This eased the Cuban state's financial burden of supporting its social, economic, and philanthropic activities.

Thus, a number of mass and front organizations that previously had been part of the central state apparatus, and that were in some instances created by and functionally tied to the Communist Party, were now converted into new NGOs eligible to receive foreign funds. These included the Federation of Cuban Women (FMC), for decades headed by Vilma Espin, Raúl Castro's wife and a member of the PCC Political Bureau; the National Association of Small Peasants (ANAP), an instrument of state agrarian policy since 1959; and the Union of Writers and Artists (UNEAC), headed by Abel Prieto, another Political Bureau member. Also receiving newly bestowed NGO status were

---

[10]Amnesty International News Service, June 20, 1995.

[11]Gunn, *Cuba's NGOs*, 1995, p. 1.

two research organizations of the Communist Party—the Center for the Study of America (CEA) and the Center for European Studies (CEE)—and *Pro-Naturaleza*, an environmental organization sponsored by the Ministry of Science, Technology, and Environment and whose leadership is employed by the ministry. Although Gunn labels these organizations "top-down NGOs," their very origins in the state and continuing ties to it disqualify them from being genuine NGOs.[12]

Gunn also identifies a number of "bottom-up NGOs" that were established through independent, individual, or community grassroots initiative. Among these are Caritas and the Pablo Milanes Foundation, founded by the popular black singer to help young artists and independent cultural institutions.

But other so-called bottom-up NGOs remain suspect because of their close ties to the state. These include the Martin Luther King Center; the Yoruba Cultural Association, whose creation in 1991 came during the government's campaign to co-opt the Babalaos of the Santería religion; and the Felix Varela Center, a foundation devoted to intellectual and humanitarian pursuits, whose director (Juan Antonio Blanco) is a former Central Committee staffer with ties to the Party and government.[13]

In fact, truly independent NGOs remain a scarce item in today's Cuba. To become a legal NGO, an organization must register with the Ministry of Justice and meet a number of criteria, many of which give government authorities the right to deny legal existence to an NGO and then to dissolve it.[14] Those organizations that may have political relevance are denied registration, except for those that were originally creatures of the state and Party—i.e., FMC, ANAP, UNEAC, CEA, and CEE—or newly established groups that have been infiltrated or co-opted by the state, such as the Martin Luther King Center and the Yoruba Cultural Association.

On the other hand, organizations whose goals are deemed to be in violation of the constitution or whose activities encroach on those of the state are denied legal status by the Ministry of Justice. Con-

---

[12]For Gunn's arguments, see Gunn, *Cuba's NGOs*, 1995, pp. 1–2.

[13]See Gunn, 1995, pp. 2–4.

[14]See Gunn, 1995, p. 3.

sequently, no opposition political parties or human-rights organizations have thus far been registered as NGOs.

Still, whether or not they are legally registered as NGOs may be of less importance than the fact that new, truly independent groups—those Gunn calls bottom-up NGOs—are forming in Cuban society despite state efforts to the contrary. An analogy would be the Cuban economy, in which the illegal black market and informal economy have begun to play a significant role, to the extent that they are displacing the public sector in many economic activities.

Thus, although they may be denied NGO status or shut down, home-based study groups and evangelical churches are growing—an encouraging sign that civil society may be gradually emerging on the island. Another encouraging sign is the emergence of the Independent Society of Cuban Economists, which, although denied status as an NGO, is able to have many of its reports reproduced on the Internet through telephone links to economists in Florida. Equally heartening is the recent creation of the Independent Press Bureau and *Concilio Cubano*. Nevertheless, the full development of civil society is likely to take years.

IMPLICATIONS FOR CUBA'S TRANSITION PROCESS

The foregoing assessment suggests that, for the short and medium terms, the primary impetus for peaceful, but fundamental, economic and political change is not likely to come from below, from Cuba's weak civil society. Rather, if such change does eventually come about, it is more likely to come from above, from Cuba's strong state, impelled by the *reformistas*. Without pressures from a more robust, assertive civil society, however, the reformers will continue to find it difficult to make their case for increasing the pace and breadth of internal reform.

As was discussed in Chapter Four, the momentum for state-driven change remains thwarted not only by Castro and the hardliners but also by the cautious, limited nature of the reforms advocated by Raúl and the centrists. Although more pragmatic than the *duros*, the *centristas* share the formers' aversion to a market economy and want instead to construct a more efficient state-run economy to retain socialism. Meanwhile, as long as civil society remains feeble and the security forces effectively control the streets, the *reformistas'* call for deeper reforms does not find a strong echo in the populace at large.

Indeed, the start-and-stop nature of Cuba's recent reforms reflects in large measure the leadership's assessment of whether the internal crisis is on the verge of spinning out of control. A flurry of reforms—the most important being the reopening and expansion of the farmers' markets—thus came on the heels of the August 1994 Havana riots and the subsequent exodus of rafters. But with social tensions subsiding, the regime has done little to maintain the pace of economic liberalization, except for the new foreign-investment law approved by the National Assembly in September 1995. The few internal reforms enacted by the regime earlier in the summer were hedged with conditions that stymie the growth of a domestic private sector.

If Cuba's modest economic recovery is not sustained, however, such a state of affairs could prove to be a recipe for disaster. With the layoff of upwards of 500,000 state workers that may need to be implemented in 1996, and with illegal out-migration having been sealed off, worsening economic conditions could trigger spontaneous, anomic-type unrest on a larger scale than the August 1994 riots. If so, Cuba would be overtaken sooner or later by political instability, increased state repression, and, perhaps, civil war.

It is possible, therefore, that Cuba's fate may already be sealed by the regime's continuing failure to enact meaningful internal reforms. Although the Castro dictatorship is an anachronism in a hemisphere that finally is becoming more democratic and market-oriented, civil unrest on the island would be damaging to U.S. interests. Such an outcome could result in the loss of Cuban lives, uncontrollable migration outflows, and increased drug-trafficking from an island that probably would be lacking in effective government. The U.S. Government would come under increased domestic pressures to intervene for humanitarian and geostrategic reasons, with possibly irreparable harm to U.S. relations with much of Latin America. The question, then, is: Can the United States do anything to hasten the process of peaceful change in Cuba without, in the process, helping Castro remain in power?

PART II: U.S. POLICY AND CUBA

Chapter Six

PRESENT U.S. POLICY AND ITS OPTIONS

What happens in Fidel Castro's Cuba over the course of the next few years will directly affect the United States. Sitting astride the Caribbean's sea-lanes of communication, Cuba commands the southern approaches to the United States. It is the Caribbean's largest island-nation, with a population of nearly 11 million. With a large concentration of Cuban-Americans in Florida, Cuba is a sensitive, often-partisan issue in American politics. The United States thus retains a legitimate, important interest in Cuba, because future developments on the island are certain to affect migration flows and drug-trafficking, and to influence domestic politics in the United States.

In the meantime, Leninist Cuba remains the region's last vestige of the Cold War. The Castro brothers and their followers cling to dogmas and political-economic formulas from another time and another place when the governments and peoples of the Caribbean and Latin America have begun to subscribe, however imperfectly, to Western principles of democracy and market-driven economies. Despite its halting efforts at change, Cuba is an anachronism in the Western Hemisphere.

Can the United States help speed the island's transition to a new Cuba that promotes the well-being of its people as well as U.S. interests and principles? The problem is that the primary determinants for political and economic change, stasis, or regression in Cuba reside in the Castro brothers, in the regime's other players, and in the island's nascent civil society. This means that whether the U.S. embargo remains in place, is tightened, or is lifted conditionally or unconditionally, U.S. policy is not likely to determine the outcome of Cuba's current transition process.

Still, U.S. policy may help to accelerate or hinder the change process by the way it (1) affects the distribution of power among regime actors, (2) provides incentives or disincentives for reform, and (3) promotes the development of civil society. Therefore, the United States' present Cuban policy and the options of tightening or ending the U.S. embargo need to be assessed in light of their effect on these three variables.

THE CUBAN DEMOCRACY ACT OF 1992

Passed overwhelmingly by Congress and signed into law by President George Bush, the Cuban Democracy Act (CDA) is the cornerstone of U.S. policy toward Cuba. The CDA seeks a "peaceful transition to democracy and a resumption of economic growth in Cuba through the careful application of sanctions directed at the Castro government and support for the Cuban people." Toward this end, Track I of the CDA seeks to close the loopholes in the embargo to increase economic pressures on the Castro dictatorship. However, the CDA allows the U.S. Government to "reduce sanctions in carefully calibrated ways in response to positive developments in Cuba."[1]

Less well known is Section 1705 of the CDA, now referred to as Track II, which stipulates measures to be taken in support of the Cuban people. Track II allows the shipment of food and medicines to Cuban individuals and NGOs, the expansion of telecommunication ties to the island, and U.S. Government assistance through NGOs to individuals and organizations in Cuba supporting peaceful democratic change.[2]

In large measure, the CDA has been a creature of American domestic politics, responding in particular to the demands of the Cuban-American community, as articulated by the Cuban-American

---

[1]The Cuban Democracy Act, Section 1703, as reprinted in The Atlantic Council of the United States, *A Road Map for Restructuring Future U.S. Relations with Cuba,* Annex A, Washington, D.C., 1995, p. 36.

[2]The Cuban Democracy Act, Section 1705, as reprinted in The Atlantic Council of the United States, *A Road Map,* 1995, pp. 37–38.

National Foundation. But Track I of the CDA has not been effective in isolating the Castro regime, because most countries have increased their trade with and investments in Cuba since the CDA became law. The embargo's porosity is why two versions of the Helms-Burton bill were passed by the House and Senate last fall.

Still, the embargo has been effective enough to irritate U.S. allies, and to incite virtually all UN members to vote against the U.S. embargo in the UN General Assembly, including in October 1995, when the vote was 117 to 3. Because it increases the costs of Cuban imports and creates uncertainty about the island's future, the embargo—or "blockade" as it is called in Cuba—has consistently been attacked by the Cuban Government. Its lifting has become Castro's number-one foreign-policy priority.

Until October 1995, Track II had been but partially implemented, and then only in the previous 12 months. Telecommunication ties with the island were improved with the Federal Communication Commission's decision in October 1994 allowing U.S. telephone companies to upgrade telephone circuits from 120 to around 700. But little else was done with Track II. Moreover, during the rafter crisis of August 1994, the president decided to ban cash remittances by Cuban-Americans to their relatives and friends on the island. This prohibition appeared to run counter to the CDA's stated goal of rendering "support to the Cuban people," because it denied the financial resources with which potential civil society actors could become independent of the state.

Track II appeared to receive another setback with the U.S.–Cuban agreement of May 2, 1995. Under it, the Clinton administration reversed long-standing U.S. policy: Henceforth, the U.S. Coast Guard was instructed to return fleeing Cubans to the Castro government to ensure orderly emigration from the island. As a result, administration critics charged that the promotion of human rights and civil society in the United States' Cuba policy had now been sacrificed to more-immediate, politically charged concerns, such as emigration.[3]

---

[3]A former Assistant Secretary of State for Latin America indicted the May 2 agreement, which was negotiated in secret, as reversing 35 years of bipartisan policy toward Castro's Cuba. The new policy of handing over Cubans to the regime, he charges, is "monstrous" and a "betrayal" of those individuals risking their lives to flee commu-

The following October, however, the White House announced new policy initiatives toward Cuba that aim at a fuller implementation of Track II. The new steps permit American news organizations to open bureaus in Havana; facilitate exchanges between American and Cuban academics, professionals, students, and clergymen; further expand telecommunication ties to the island; facilitate the purchase of fax machines and computer equipment by Cubans; permit funding of newly emergent Cuban NGOs by U.S.–based NGOs; and ease travel restrictions on Cuban-Americans who visit relatives on the island.[4] These measures constitute an effort to reach out to and support civil society actors on the island through increased information and money flows, and people-to-people contacts.

In the meantime, however porous it may be, the embargo constitutes one of the few sources of political and economic leverage that the U.S. Government has in dealing with Castro. Its easing under a "calibrated response" policy or its lifting altogether through a final negotiated settlement is seen as the primary instrument by which the United States can help move Cuba toward a more democratic and market-based system.[5] It also remains a trump card for the U.S. Government in negotiating a settlement with Cuba for the $1.8 billion in property claims by American individuals and corporations, resulting from the Castro government's expropriations, that were certified as valid by the U.S. Foreign Claims Settlement Commission. With the simple interest specified by the 1964 Cuban Claims Act, these original claims now amount to about $5.8 billion.

---

nism. The agreement, he claims, is but the first step by the administration "to apologize for the embargo and adopt a more 'mature' policy" toward the Castro government. See Elliot Abrams, "Castro's Latest Coup," *National Review*, June 12, 1995, pp. 36–37.

[4]These policy initiatives had been in the works for some time. Their implementation by a Presidential Executive Order reportedly had been delayed over concern that, on the heels of the May 2 immigration agreement, Cuban-American groups and congressional Republicans would attack the new moves as steps toward normalization of relations. See Steven Greenhouse, "To Undermine Castro, U.S. Planning Wider Links with Cubans," *The New York Times*, June 12, 1995, p. A6.

[5]The Inter-American Dialogue, for example, noted that "the embargo can serve as a practical element of policy, if it is used as a bargaining chip in negotiations with Cuba. . . . The U.S. government should be prepared, step by step, to lift its trade embargo in response to specific initiatives taken by the Cuban government." Inter-American Dialogue, *Cuba in the Americas*, 1995, p. ii.

Because of the CDA's provisions, the Castro government's authoritarian character and state-controlled economy stand as major impediments to lifting the embargo and resuming normalized relations. As a recent Atlantic Council study points out, the president has the unilateral authority to extend diplomatic recognition to Cuba, because such an act lies within the purview of the Executive Branch. With respect to the embargo, however, the Cuban Democracy Act stipulates that the president must first make a determination and then report to Congress that the Cuban Government has held fair, internationally supervised elections, is observing human rights, and is moving toward a market economy, among other things, before the sanctions against Cuba can be removed.[6]

THE PROS AND CONS OF THE EMBARGO

What to do about the U.S. embargo became an increasing source of controversy following the August 1994 riots and subsequent immigration crisis. Concerned that social tensions on the island could explode, with adverse consequences for the United States, especially Florida, foreign-policy advisers, congressmen, and op-ed writers began urging that it be lifted to achieve a "soft landing" in Castro's Cuba in order to ensure the island's peaceful transition and stability.[7] Since then, businessmen wanting to trade with and invest in Cuba have added their voice to the growing chorus calling for lifting the embargo.

But there are also those in and outside the U.S. Government who favor retaining the embargo as strengthened by the CDA. They argue that the embargo should not be lifted until Cuba undergoes more-fundamental political and economic change. To lift the embargo unconditionally, they maintain, would remove a major inducement to the regime for deepening the reform process. In this respect, they point out that the embargo has not failed as its critics allege; rather, it

---

[6]The Atlantic Council of the United States, *A Road Map*, 1995, p. 3. This certification requirement is contained in Section 1708 of the Cuban Democracy Act.

[7]For early examples by those influential in the foreign-policy community, see Zbigniew Brzezinski, "Facing Up to Consequences of a Castro Crash Landing," *Los Angeles Times*, September 7, 1994; and Claiborne Pell and Lee H. Hamilton, "The Embargo Must Go," *The Washington Post*, September 8, 1994.

has been a factor forcing the regime to undertake the economy's partial liberalization.[8]

Still others in the Republican-controlled House and Senate want to hasten Castro's downfall and Cuba's transition to democracy by seeking the island's virtual economic isolation. The Cuban Liberty and Democracy Act, introduced by Senator Jesse Helms and Representative Dan Burton, thus goes further than the CDA. As originally conceived, the Helms-Burton bill would continue U.S. opposition to the giving of aid and loans to Cuba by international agencies and would allow the president to cut foreign aid to Russia if the latter provides economic assistance to Cuba. It would impose punitive sanctions on third countries, their business firms, and their business representatives who violate the embargo. And in its most controversial provision, it would allow Cuban-Americans whose properties had been expropriated to file lawsuits in U.S. courts, demanding billions of dollars in compensation not only from the Cuban Government but also from foreign companies that use expropriated assets on the island.[9]

On the other hand, the original Helms-Burton bill also held out a carrot for a "new Cuba." Thus, the embargo would be eased if a transitional government in Havana planned "free and fair elections" within a year, provided that such a government did not include either of the Castro brothers and that the present organs of state repression were dissolved.

In September and October 1995, the House and Senate passed two versions of the Helms-Burton bill, with the Senate's being a watered-

---

[8]This is the position adopted by Gonzalez and Ronfeldt, *Storm Warnings for Cuba,* 1994.

[9]This last provision of the Helms-Burton bill appears to be in violation of international law, because it allows Cuban-Americans to sue for compensation in American courts even though they were not American citizens at the time their property was confiscated. The inclusion of Cuban-American claims would greatly increase the amount of compensation demanded, from $5.8 billion in certified claims for U.S. firms and individuals, to an estimated additional $20 billion in claims for Cuban-Americans. This would make it harder for the American claimants to obtain full payment from the Castro government or its successor, given Cuba's limited resources.

down version of the original legislation.[10] The Senate eliminated the controversial claims provision that favored Cuban-Americans. It dropped the provision that would bar executives and shareholders from foreign corporations that had invested in Cuba from entering the United States. It also allowed the transitional government to convene elections within two years rather than the one year stipulated in the House bill.

Although the House version is tougher, it holds out an important carrot for Cuba not found in the Senate's version: To help prepare the Cuban armed forces to adjust to their "appropriate role" in a future democracy, it contains a Military Adjustment Provision that commits the United States to providing military assistance to both a transitional government and an elected one.

As of the beginning of December 1995, the House and Senate versions remained to be reconciled in a conference committee. Even then, the bill may be vetoed by the president, with an override vote by the Senate considered doubtful.

Maintaining or Tightening the Embargo

The argument for maintaining the present embargo, as modified by the Cuban Democracy Act of 1992, can be summarized as follows:

- With the collapse of the Soviet Union, the U.S. embargo has become more effective than ever, as evidenced not only by Cuba's severe economic crisis but also by the fact that Castro has made lifting the embargo his regime's top foreign-policy priority.

- This is not the time to lift the embargo; the regime is on the ropes and "Castro's days are numbered."[11]

---

[10]In September, the House passed the bill by a vote of 294 to 130; the Senate passed its version of the bill in late October by a vote of 74 to 24. For a concise summary of the two versions, see "Senate Approves Weak Helms-Burton Law," and "The House Version: A Lot Tougher," *CubaNews*, November 1995, p. 7.

[11]See the full-page advertisement by prominent Republicans and others, "An Open Letter to the President of the United States: Castro's Days Are Numbered—Don't Bail Out a Failed Dictator!" *The New York Times*, September 26, 1994.

- Because of the worsening economic crisis, to which the embargo has contributed, the regime has had to introduce more market-type reforms over the past three years than at any time since Castro took power.

It therefore follows that, before the embargo is eased or lifted, the evidence should be clear that the reform process in Cuba is deep and irreversible.[12]

The supporters of the Helms-Burton bill go further in insisting on the need to ratchet up the pressures on the Castro dictatorship by blocking aid and loans to Cuba by international agencies, and by discouraging foreign corporations from investing in Cuba. Because of the additional economic deprivation that Cuba would experience, either the regime would be forced to implement meaningful political and economic reforms to save itself, something that Helms-Burton's main proponents doubt would occur, or, in the absence of such reforms, the island's worsening economic situation would eventually lead to the regime's ouster from power, which is the goal of the bill's most avid supporters.

Lifting the Embargo

The argument for the conditional or unconditional lifting of the embargo rests on the premise that the embargo is a relic of the Cold War, that the 33-year-old policy has failed to topple the Castro regime, and that its continued implementation only hurts the Cuban people, not the regime—indeed, the latter gains from it politically. According to this argument, lifting the embargo is likely to produce desired changes in Cuba by doing the following:

- Eliminating the United States as an external threat against which Castro has rallied nationalistic Cubans in support of his rule

- Depriving Castro of an external scapegoat for the economic crisis, which is largely a product of his own short-sighted and mistaken policies

---

[12]This was one of the recommendations made by Gonzalez and Ronfeldt, *Storm Warnings for Cuba*, 1994.

- Lifting the regime's siege mentality and thereby providing needed political space within which political liberalization and market reforms can take place

- Allowing trade and foreign investments to impel economic change on the island

- Increasing the Cuban people's contacts with American tourists, businessmen, clergymen, students, and academics, which would eventually corrode the regime's control over society.

The cumulative effect of these developments, it is believed, would promote the forces of reform in Cuba—or perhaps even lead to the demise of the Castro regime.

Those who call for the embargo's lifting usually cite the moderating or unsettling effects that increased engagement with the West had on Eastern Europe, China, and, perhaps now, Vietnam. If the lifting were followed by the resumption of full diplomatic relations, then the United States would have an even greater presence with which to influence developments on the island.

THE ARGUMENTS REVISITED

Proponents for lifting or tightening the embargo often exaggerate the extent to which U.S. policy determines Cuba's future course. Also, they ignore how each of their policies may play out in Cuba, particularly how each could affect the distribution of power within the regime. The errors in their arguments, discussed below, fall into three categories: drawing inappropriate analogies, underestimating the regime's staying power, and ignoring how a policy may play out in Cuba.

Error 1: Drawing Inappropriate Analogies

One major flaw in the argument calling for the lifting of the embargo is that it rests on the premise that the experience the West has had with communist states in Eastern Europe and Asia is the same as that with Cuba. But Cuba is a *sui generis* case in which analogies drawn from other countries do not necessarily apply. In contrast to the weak, illegitimate communist regimes of Eastern Europe, Cuba experienced an indigenous revolution led by a genuine national hero who invested the regime with intrinsic legitimacy. Today, it has a much stronger state and a weaker civil society than existed in most of the former East European communist states, as evidenced by the fact that the Castro regime remains entrenched despite the Soviet Union's disappearance in 1991.[13]

Comparisons with current "reformed" communist regimes in China and Vietnam also do not hold: Cuba's economic liberalization is not nearly as far along as was China's when Washington restored full diplomatic relations with Beijing or Vietnam's when the U.S. embargo was lifted in 1994, which was then followed by the restoration of diplomatic relations in July 1995. Moreover, both the Chinese and Vietnamese regimes remain politically repressive Leninist regimes, despite their economic opening to the West. Unlike China and Vietnam, however, Cuba's authoritarian system presents an obstacle to the lifting of the embargo because of the CDA's certification requirements that Cuba have held democratic elections.

To be sure, the embargo's lifting may have the corrosive effect on Cuban society that many predict. But it still may take years before the regime itself and the power that the Cuban state wields over society are severely weakened. After all, it took decades of internal decay and exposure to the West before the widely despised, illegitimate communist regimes of Eastern Europe, which owed their power to the Red Army, started to crumble. Even then, it took Soviet disengagement from the region to give decisive impetus to the process of decomposition.

Castro knows that Cuba is different from Eastern Europe. That is why he has made the embargo's lifting his number-one foreign-policy priority. He has more confidence than do some U.S. policy critics that his regime can withstand the corrosive effects of the embargo's lifting on society while benefiting from the new infusion of American tourist and investment dollars.

---

[13]For a fuller analysis of the similarities and differences between Cuba and Eastern Europe, see Michael Radu, "Cuba's Transition: Institutional Lessons from Eastern Europe," *Journal of Interamerican Studies and World Affairs*, Vol. 37, No. 2, Summer 1995, pp. 83–111.

Error 2: Underestimating the Regime's Staying Power

As with the case for lifting the embargo, the Helms-Burton bill also rests on much the same dubious premise that the Castro regime is as weak and sclerotic as were the East European communist states. The bill would thus increase pressures to speed Castro's inevitable demise.

The problem is that the Castro regime has demonstrated an extraordinary resiliency in coping not only with the "first embargo" imposed by the United States in 1962 but also in surviving the "second embargo" caused by the disappearance of the Soviet Union in 1991. To be sure, the regime may still founder in the not-too-distant future. But the fact remains that the regime has thus far not followed in the footsteps of its erstwhile communist allies in Eastern Europe—precisely because it is different from them: different in its authentic revolutionary origins; in its indigenous, nationalist character; in its popular and, for some, still-charismatic leader; and in its stronger state and weaker civil society.

Error 3: Ignoring How a Policy May Play Out in Cuba

Proponents arguing for either the lifting or tightening of the embargo have made assumptions concerning expected outcomes that, in turn, justify their policy. Thus, it is assumed that lifting the embargo will have a moderating effect on the Cuban leadership and thereby facilitate change; conversely, it is assumed that the embargo's tightening will lead to Castro's downfall. But neither of these outcomes can be predicted with any certainty unless we know how the policy in question is likely to affect the internal distribution of power among key players in Cuba: Will the policy strengthen or weaken the hand of Fidel, Raúl, the *duros*, *centristas*, or *reformistas*? How will it affect civil society actors?

As will be seen in the next chapter, current policy in some ways works to Castro's advantage and helps maintain the present internal distribution of power in Cuba. However, the alternatives of tightening or lifting the embargo could potentially have even more perverse consequences—strengthening the Castro leadership and Cuba's strong state while hurting or only minimally aiding civil society.

Chapter Seven

U.S. POLICY OPTIONS AND CUBAN FUTURES

How a given U.S. policy may help or hinder fundamental system change in Cuba hinges upon whether it strengthens or weakens those Cuban actors, in and outside the regime, who are committed to genuine political and economic reforms. It is possible that a policy could work to Castro's immediate political and economic advantage, yet strengthen both the regime's reformers and civil society over the longer run. Hence, the following analysis will differentiate between the effects of different policy options on the internal distribution of power in Cuba and, thus, on the change process itself, according to the short term (1 year), medium term (1–3 years), and long term (beyond 3 years).

STAYING THE COURSE

As noted in Chapter Six, present policy is based on the Cuban Democracy Act of 1992. As of this writing, it includes the Track II initiatives adopted by the administration in October 1995, but not the provisions of the Helms-Burton bill, which remains to be reconciled by a House-Senate conference committee and which may be vetoed by the president.

On the economic side, for the short to medium term, the present policy denies the Castro regime the U.S. tourist and investment dollars that could ensure its survival. Although not effective in isolating Cuba from the world economy, the embargo compounds the economic problems that the regime must overcome. By so doing, the embargo increases the necessity for internal economic changes, thereby strengthening the position of the *centristas* and *reformistas*.

Consequently, if current U.S. policy is maintained over the next year or two, Cuba is likely to continue adopting some limited market-type reforms, principally in the external sector of the economy, but with the economy remaining state-directed and without much privatization, except in its foreign enclaves. Because Raúl and the *centristas*, not the *reformistas*, are the ones leading this "reform" process, the regime would continue adhering to a market-Leninist model—a model that is more Leninist than market-oriented.

In the political sphere, the current policy strengthens the hand of both the *centristas* and *duros*, and their determination to retain the regime's Leninist character. The CDA enables Castro to displace much of the blame for Cuba's economic ills onto an external enemy, mobilize the populace behind the regime on the basis of nationalism, and justify Cuba's garrison state and vanguard Communist Party. Present policy also serves to coalesce different regime elites around the Castro brothers as the only alternative to regime collapse, chaos, and possible civil war.

Now that Track II has begun to be more fully implemented, current policy may nurture civil society more actively than in the past. Such nurturance could assist the Catholic Church and Protestant denominations, and their affiliated lay groups, in the immediate future. As a result, more-robust civil society actors may emerge over the longer term, provided they are not tainted by their funding or other ties to U.S. NGOs.

However, because the ban on remittances by Cuban exiles has not been rescinded, individual Cubans may continue to find it difficult to gain independence from the state. Present policy also does not reach out to the younger generation of civilian and military leaders, who may be more flexible and less anti-American in their attitude. It does not exploit the regime's existing or potential fault lines between or among military and civilian elites, or between the younger generation of reformers and older, more hardline elements.

Except for the new Track II initiatives, therefore, current U.S. policy does little to directly promote Cuba's political and economic liberalization. By compounding the island's economic difficulties, however, present policy does help indirectly to create conditions that have obliged the regime to undertake some reforms. But this gain is offset by the political effect that present policy has on the Cuban leadership. By increasing threat perception, the policy resonates with those elite circles—i.e., the *duros* and *centristas*—that most favor market-Leninism.

Ultimately, the market-Leninist model may enable the regime to muddle through, provided it can get through the current crisis over the next year or two. On the other hand, the model's intrinsic limitations and contradictions may prevent the island's economic recovery over the medium term. This failure could lead to growing political instability, resulting in heightened state repression or possibly violent upheaval.

TIGHTENING THE EMBARGO UNDER HELMS-BURTON

Tightening the embargo as proposed by the Helms-Burton bill could result in an immediate economic setback for Cuba because of the punitive sanctions that the United States would impose on foreign governments, corporations, and business executives who are trading and investing in Cuba. Prior to the bill's passage in the House and Senate, there were some signs that investments had begun to slow. But as 1995 drew to a close, this situation was no longer apparent, perhaps because of Cuba's new foreign-investment law and signs of long-term stability.

If Helms-Burton does become law, Canada, Spain, England, Mexico, Japan, and other countries could curtail their exposure in Cuba to appease Washington. Conversely, they could challenge the extraterritorial reach of the new U.S. policy on grounds that the provisions of Helms-Burton violate their states' sovereignty and international law. In either case, the new policy would entail high diplomatic and political costs for the United States from damaged relations with other countries.

Although it may hurt Cuba economically, Helms-Burton would work to the regime's political advantage in the short to medium terms. Castro is at his best in playing upon Cuban nationalism and attacking the efforts of the "empire" to "strangle" Cuba economically. Because the bill's original version—approved by the House—supported compensation for expropriated properties belonging to Cuban-Americans, Helms-Burton enables Castro and his regime to heighten widespread fears of dispossession and future impoverishment among the Cuban people. With Helms-Burton trying to "destroy the Revolution," Castro and the hardliners are also able to justify their insistence on maintaining authoritarianism and heavy-handed repression against dissidents and human-rights activists. Thus, since early 1995, the government has been waging a public campaign to rekindle internal support and international solidarity in the struggle against Helms-Burton.

Helms-Burton also helps Castro maintain regime cohesion despite its overtures to the regime's non-*fidelista* and -*raulista* elites. Both versions of the bill state that the U.S. Government will be impartial toward the makeup of a newly elected post-Castro government, provided neither Fidel nor Raúl Castro is in it and the present organs of state repression are dissolved. The House bill also stipulates that U.S. military assistance will be given to the armed forces in a post-Castro democratic Cuba.

The trouble with these stipulations is that Helms-Burton sends mixed signals to Cuba's current political elites:

- On the one hand, most members of the regime are told that they need not fear being purged in a post-Castro Cuba, and there is also the prospect of future assistance to a reconstituted Cuban military.

- On the other hand, Helms-Burton aims at increasing economic pressures and isolating Cuba to bring about the Castro regime's downfall—an objective that poses an immediate, palpable threat to all military and civilian elites, whether they are hardliners, centrists, or reformers.

Hence, as already has occurred, Helms-Burton further solidifies the regime around the Castro brothers instead of exacerbating internal leadership divisions.

What would the likely long-term consequences of this new policy be? If it is effective in curtailing foreign trade and investments, the island's economic recovery would be precluded, living conditions would deteriorate, and social tensions would increase. Such deterioration could lead to the regime's eventual overthrow as envisaged by the framers of Helms-Burton.

On the other hand, growing internal disorder could give the upper hand to Castro, the *duros*, and the internal security apparatus. Unlike most of the *reformistas* and some *centristas*, they would be prepared to use whatever force is necessary to remain in power. At least for the short to medium term, therefore, the policy would strengthen those leadership circles and state institutions most opposed to political and economic change.

Meanwhile, Helms-Burton is likely to stunt further development of civil society. The current ban on cash remittances to Cubans on the island would probably remain in place to deny the regime access to dollars. Promoting greater information flows and people-to-people contacts would become more difficult, given restrictions by both the U.S. and Cuban governments. If deprived of external sources of support from the United States, financial or otherwise, Cuba's civil society actors would have to depend exclusively on their ties to Western Europe and possibly Latin America. With the possible exception of the Catholic Church and some Protestant churches, the ranks of civil society would remain thin and unable to effectively press for change from below.

In sum, the new policy would strengthen the hand of the most-recalcitrant regime actors, those opposed to economic and political liberalization, while leaving civil society in its present feeble state. Were the embargo to curtail new foreign investments and trade, the island's economic situation would deteriorate. Economic deterioration could lead to violent upheaval and the regime's eventual undoing—or to the regime's remaining entrenched during a protracted period of heightened political instability, tighter state repression, and uncontrolled out-migration.

LIFTING THE EMBARGO

It is unlikely that the Clinton administration would consider lifting the embargo before the 1996 presidential elections. Such a policy reversal is made more difficult by the CDA's requirement that Cuba must first have held free, democratic elections and must respect human rights before the embargo can be lifted. Nevertheless, the potential consequences of the embargo's being lifted need to be assessed because it is a policy option that continues to be advanced by some members of Congress, by conservative as well as liberal commentators, and in academic and business circles. Relaxation of the embargo is also advocated by most Western states. Two variants of this policy option are considered below under two reasonably credible scenarios.

Scenario 1: Lifting the Embargo Without Conditions

Suppose that, after the 1996 elections, U.S. policy toward Cuba is reassessed. The new administration determines that the Castro government is continuing to implement modest economic reforms and that the regime's permanency appears ensured. Policymakers conclude that the embargo is both ineffective and a major source of friction with U.S. allies, that it impedes further economic liberalization in Cuba, that it shuts out American business interests, and that it provides Castro with an excuse to maintain his hard line toward political dissidents and human-rights activists.

Secret negotiations are held between Washington and Havana. The president establishes diplomatic relations with the Castro government. In return, Havana pledges its commitment to additional economic reforms, the release of political prisoners, greater political space for dissent, and unrestricted travel by Cubans to the United States and by Cuban exiles and Americans to the island. However, Cuban authorities insist that these are domestic issues that remain solely within Cuba's jurisdiction as an independent and sovereign country. After congressional debate, the embargo is lifted unconditionally, but only after the Cuban Government's announcement that it agrees to establishing a joint commission to settle the claims issue.

With normalization and the embargo's lifting, relations between the two countries are stabilized. Stabilization reassures Canada, Western Europe, and others that they can now increase their economic stake in Cuba, including extending new loans and credits. Meanwhile, Cuban-Americans, American tourists, and U.S. corporate investors flock to the island. As a consequence, economic conditions on the island improve markedly, and flows of information and people in and out of the country increase significantly.

How is this U.S. policy shift, together with its likely repercussions, likely to play out in Cuba? The consequences for the short to medium terms would be different from those for the longer term.

Over both the short and medium terms, the unconditional lifting of the embargo would strengthen Castro's power and stature within his regime. His admirers have always been in awe of him because of his success as an audacious, cunning, and far-sighted leader. Time and again they have seen him steer Cuba's ship of state into perilous waters, only to have it reemerge stronger than ever—and in safe waters. Hence, they would view the lifting of the embargo as a new triumph for Fidel, one that would enable him to avert the catastrophe that they feared had been awaiting Cuba since the collapse of the Soviet Union. Thus, his indispensability as supreme leader would be reaffirmed within the regime.

Meanwhile, the infusion of American tourists and investments would provide Castro with the dollars for easing Cuba's economic crisis and repaying European lenders and creditors, without having to enact market reforms for the internal economy. Not having made a binding commitment to liberalizing the economy, he could stall, dilute, or postpone new market reforms. Or, as is currently the case, he could limit the reforms to foreign investors, with the expectation that such a step would be sufficient to defuse international criticism of his policies while continuing to attract new foreign capital.

This is not idle speculation. That the momentum for reform would be set back by the embargo's lifting has been recently confirmed by Castro's behavior following developments in October 1995 that seem to signal clear sailing for his regime. Larry Rohter, *The New York Times* correspondent in Havana, reported that Castro and his followers, buoyed by his public-relations success in New York, growing foreign-investor interest in Cuba, and signs of the island's improving economy, "seem to have drawn a singular lesson from their recent successes: Perhaps there is no further need for their regime to loosen up, either toward political freedom, or toward more open markets." One foreign diplomat was quoted as saying that the Cuban Government is "once again acting in a triumphalist manner," while another diplomat observed that

> they seem to be drawing the wrong lesson from what has happened. Instead of looking on the promising results they have obtained thus

far as a signal to press on even further, they appear to be telling themselves that they have now done all they need to get by.[1]

In both the short and medium term, therefore, lifting the embargo unconditionally would convince Castro, the hardliners, and the centrists that no further economic or political changes were necessary. The new U.S. policy would undercut the position of the *reformistas*, because Cuba's economic crisis could be overcome without having to enact deeper reforms.

Meanwhile, the island's growing economic ties to the United States and the West would not necessarily abate the regime's authoritarian character. As Latin America, China, and Southeast Asia have demonstrated, regimes with even more-abysmal human-rights records than Cuba's can continue to attract both foreign tourists and investments. For a while, at least, Cuba could remain a market-Leninist state—one that uses foreign capital to avoid having to create a market economy.

For the longer term, however, the embargo's lifting might eventually weaken the regime by setting in motion societal forces that it could not control. Greater flows of people, information, cash remittances, and NGO funds to the island would help nourish civil society, as would more opportunities for Cubans to travel abroad. The requirements of American and other Western firms for unrestricted access to the labor force, internal market, and decentralized computer and telecommunication networks, and for supportive, contractual linkages with a Cuban private sector, would begin to erode the state's control over the economy and society.

These and other trends would in time help the *reformista*s, enabling them to find external support among increasingly important civil society actors—not only churches but also student and academic circles, independent trade unions, professional groups, and private entrepreneurs. Thus buttressed from below, the regime's reformists might eventually be able to push for renewed economic and political reforms on grounds of maintaining economic growth and strengthening regime legitimacy.

---

[1]Larry Rohter, "A Little Hope," 1995, p. 3.

However, this transition to a more democratic as well as market-oriented order could take years. It probably would also depend on whether the Castro brothers, especially Fidel, remained at the helm of Cuba's ship of state. If one or both were still in charge, the transition would most likely remain far in the distant future.

Scenario 2: Lifting the Embargo with Conditions

The more credible policy option would be for the embargo to be lifted with conditions agreed to by the Castro regime. This option might unfold along lines of the following scenario, again after the 1996 elections, and in the context of Cuba's worsening economic situation.

The embargo's lifting would be tied to the Cuban Government's pledge to hold free and internationally supervised elections, as well as to abide by other conditions stipulated in the CDA that would level the playing field for newly created opposition parties. Such a package could be brokered by the Spanish government because of its interest in protecting Spain's economic stake in the island and in furthering Spain's special relationship with Latin America.

However, although it wants the embargo lifted, the Castro government has time and again rejected internationally supervised elections as an infringement of Cuban sovereignty and as unnecessary because Cuba already has "real democracy." Moreover, Castro and other Cuban leaders are well aware of the political risks they would take in holding fair elections, in which opposition parties could compete for votes at a time when the Cuban people have had to endure a severe drop in their standard of living. Six years earlier, in fact, they had advised the *Sandinistas* not to commit themselves to internationally supervised elections for the same reason.

Nevertheless, the Cuban leadership now concludes that there is no other way out of Cuba's economic morass except to accept the package deal proposed by Spanish mediators. But Castro insists on and obtains three key concessions: that the embargo be eased prior to the elections, that his government remain in office through the elections, and that the elections be held within a relatively short period—perhaps 12 or, at most, 15 months.

Under this formula, Cuba would appear to be moving toward a Nicaraguan-type solution. In that war-torn country, the February 1990 internationally supervised elections led to the defeat of President Daniel Ortega and the *Sandinistas* at the hands of Violeta Chamorro and a broad opposition coalition.

Would Cuba be a repeat of Nicaragua? Assuming that Castro is eligible and decides to run for office, as Ortega did in Nicaragua, two divergent outcomes appear possible. In the first, Castro and the Communist Party win the elections; in the second, the opposition wins.

Castro Wins. As with Nicaragua under *Sandinista* rule, economic conditions in Cuba have been terrible, while decades of hardship and unfulfilled promises have alienated much of the Cuban population from the Castro regime. Still, if elections were convened within a relatively short period, the *fidelistas* might conceivably win. One reason this may happen is that Fidel Castro is not Daniel Ortega. But another, equally important reason is that Castro's Cuba differs from *Sandinistas'* Nicaragua.

Cuba has less of a civil society than existed in Nicaragua under the *Sandinistas*. Throughout the decade of *Sandinista* rule in Nicaragua, the Catholic Church remained a popular national institution that wielded political power. A large private sector continued to exist under a mixed economy in which state control was never total nor effective. And, although harassed by the regime, opposition political parties, together with an independent press and labor unions, continued to function under *Sandinista* rule.

This structure of organized, institutionalized opposition to a revolutionary Marxist government has been missing for decades in Cuba. It cannot be created overnight. It may well take years to develop.

Thus, because they would only now be coming into existence following the agreement on internationally supervised elections, newly created opposition parties on the island would probably be disorganized and fragmented. As with many dissident and opposition groups today, they probably would be divided by ideological, generational, and racial differences. The likelihood is that they would also be less skilled in political combat than were their Nicaraguan counterparts.

Against his opposition, Castro would have a formidable mobi-lizational apparatus for getting out the vote. Controlled by the Communist Party, the apparatus includes the Committees for the Defense of the Revolution, the Cuban Confederation of Workers, the Federation of Cuban Women, and other mass organizations operat-ing at the grass-roots level. Meanwhile, the improvement in eco-nomic conditions that came with the embargo's gradual lifting could well revive popular support for Cuba's *lider máximo*. His appeal could be further strengthened if opposition parties, because of their squabbling, appeared incapable of governing or if they were viewed as opposed to the Revolution's social gains.

What would be the likely short- to medium-term consequences of a Castro victory at the polls? The elections would confer needed legit-imacy on his regime at home and abroad, help attract new foreign investments, and deprive the Communist Party of its Leninist van-guard role and monopoly of political power. Still, the electoral out-come would consolidate the power and authority of a leadership that remains profoundly antidemocratic and opposed to a market econ-omy.

The medium- if not longer-term consequence of a Castro victory would probably be a Cuba that is only quasi-democratic, much like Mexico under the rule of the Institutional Revolutionary Party (PRI). If U.S. tourist and investment dollars pour into Cuba, the govern-ment would have the resources with which to ease the island's eco-nomic crisis and perpetuate its power, without having to marketize—much less privatize—major portions of the domestic sector of the economy. Under this scenario, Cuba would, in essence, begin to catch up to the state-centric, authoritarian systems found in Mexico and other Latin American countries in the 1960s and 1970s. As with those systems, the evolution toward an institutionalized democracy and a market economy might have to await the passage of decades.

The Opposition Wins. Because of the regime's tight grip on society, no one really knows, including the Cuban people themselves, the extent to which the populace is alienated from and in opposition to the Castro regime. Now, with international monitors present, anti-Castro political parties gain access to the media, aggressively attack the regime's record, and attract widespread popular support. As oc-curred in the 1990 Nicaraguan elections, when voters finally realized that they could vote their conscience without fear of *Sandinista* retaliation, Cubans vote Castro and his government out of office.

Despite their defeat at the polls, however, the Castro brothers, their followers, and the Communist Party would most probably follow the *Sandinista* example of "governing from below" in post-1990 Nicaragua. There, the Sandinista National Liberation Front retains a sizable united bloc in the new National Assembly while controlling trade unions, other mass organizations, and the Army. Thus, while giving up the presidency and formal control of the government, the *Sandinistas* continued their political struggle by shifting it to the streets and blocking the Executive in the legislature.

The same could occur in a post-Castro Cuba. The election outcome would result in the presidency, machinery of government, and much of congress being in the hands of the anti-Castro forces. On the other hand, the Cuban military would remain a bastion of *fidelista* and *raulista* influence and, thus, a threat to the new government, despite efforts to de-politicize the Army, which is what happened in Nicaragua.[2] And if it held a bloc of seats in the new legislature, the Communist Party could maneuver to block legislation.

Meanwhile, because its cadres control much of organized labor and other mass organizations, the Communist Party, through strikes and popular demonstrations, would be in a position to block the new government. By thus threatening to render Cuba ungovernable, the PCC could seek power-sharing concessions from the new government while impressing upon the general populace that only the ousted *fidelista-raulista* leadership was capable of governing and ensuring public order. As a consequence, the new Cuba would probably continue to experience considerable political turbulence.

Nevertheless, this election outcome would probably result in a government that would be far more democratic and market-oriented than one under the Castro leadership. Over the medium term, if not longer, it would provide the political space and civility within which

---

[2]In Nicaragua, it took five years after Chamorro's victory before Gen. Humberto Ortega Savedra, brother of Daniel, stepped down as Defense Minister and chief of the Sandinista People's Army, posts he had held for 11 years of *Sandinista* rule. He was succeeded by Gen. Joaquin Caudra Lacayo, also a *Sandinista* military officer. *The New York Times*, July 16, 1995, p. 5.

a more vibrant civil society could begin to emerge. Because the new government would move quickly to embrace a market economy, it would not only attract more foreign capital but also actively promote the development of a flourishing private sector in the domestic economy.

ASSESSING THE FOUR POLICIES AND THEIR OUTCOMES

The foregoing suggests that it will be difficult to obtain a soft landing in Cuba even under the best of policy outcomes. On the other hand, some outcomes appear potentially less damaging or more favorable to U.S. interests than others.

For the time being, staying the course appears to be a prudent policy for the United States, because Cuba remains in flux. Under market-Leninism, the island continues to be opened up to foreign capital, and the regime thus far has succeeded in maintaining tight control over society. Although there are some signs of recovery, the economic outlook remains uncertain and, as a result, the political situation could become more volatile. Meanwhile, as Castro made abundantly clear by his July 26 speech, and by his more recent statements and actions, his regime will neither adopt market reforms for the internal economy nor open up the polity. Vietnam, not the market democracies of the West, is his model.

Hence, until Cuba's reform process is deepened and becomes irreversible, present policy as defined by the Cuban Democracy Act is a prudent course for the United States to follow. The CDA provides both the leverage and the flexibility with which to influence Cuba's hoped-for transition toward a democratic, market-oriented society. Still, present policy could be strengthened by expanding and more fully implementing Track II of the CDA while also taking bolder steps to exploit leadership divisions within the regime.

Imperfect as it is, current policy resonates with the core democratic values and market principles subscribed to by the United States. After decades of authoritarianism and state-dominated economies, nations in Latin America and the Caribbean are finally adopting these same values and principles. To accept Cuba's Vietnamization would thus be to hold Cuba to a lower standard than other countries in the region, including Haiti.

However, present policy may not be sustainable over the longer term. There is a breakdown in policy consensus over Cuba in the American body politic. This breakdown is made evident by those in Congress who want to tighten or lift the embargo, by newspaper editorials calling for the embargo's easing, by growing interest on the part of some sectors of the U.S. business community in trade with and investment in Cuba, and by the increasing number of Americans who violate federal regulations by traveling to Cuba. There is also international criticism of the U.S. embargo. Meanwhile, as U.S. policy comes under increased criticism, the Castro regime continues to sail on.

Turning up economic pressures, as proposed by the Helms-Burton bill, would probably hurt the regime severely and could lead to the regime's eventual undoing—or to protracted instability, higher levels of repression by an entrenched Castro regime, and, possibly, U.S. armed intervention to remove the regime and restore order on the island. Under either outcome, this policy option would hurt the Cuban people, would do little to promote either civil society or divisions in the internal elite, and would enable Castro to garner nationalist support at home and international solidarity abroad. If diligently implemented, it would upset relations with U.S. allies. Were it to cause the collapse of the Castro government, its very success could set back relations with Latin America, as occurred following the CIA-engineered ouster of the Arbenz government in Guatemala in 1954. And that success could undermine the legitimacy of post-Castro governments.

On balance, then, the Helms-Burton policy might result in Castro's downfall over the medium to longer terms. But this outcome is by no means certain. The same policy could lead to alternative worst-case scenarios: growing civil strife, state repression, and direct U.S. intervention. Even were the regime to succumb, the costs would likely be high for both the United States and Cuba long after Castro's demise.

Lifting the embargo without conditions also appears shortsighted. Such a policy reversal would greatly strengthen Castro's position within and outside his regime. It would weaken the position of the *reformistas* by giving him, and other like-minded leaders opposed to liberalization, the tourist and investment dollars with which to overcome the island's crisis without implementing deeper reforms.

Meanwhile, the government would remain authoritarian, although perhaps less outwardly repressive because of improved economic conditions.

For the short- to medium-term, this policy option would thus ensure Cuba's authoritarianism as a market-Leninist state—in effect, a Caribbean version of Vietnam. Over the longer term, this policy might eventually set in motion uncontrollable societal forces that would strengthen the position of the *reformista*s. But whether this strengthening would lead to fundamental system change toward democracy and a market economy would depend on whether the Castro brothers are still running Cuba.

Lifting the embargo in return for Castro holding internationally supervised elections does provide a peaceful mechanism for advancing system change. However, the feasibility of this option depends on such a sharp deterioration in the island's economic situation that Castro has no alternative but to accept the proposed *quid pro quo*. So far, this prerequisite has not appeared on the horizon. But were conditions to change, two outcomes would be possible under this option.

Were Castro and his Communist Party to win, the elections would legitimize and strengthen an antidemocratic, antimarket regime. Even so, some political space would have been created for civil society, and the Castro regime could no longer be Leninist. Instead, it might come to resemble Mexico's authoritarian regime of decades past.

Were Castro and his Communist Party to lose, the elections would put Cuba on the road toward democracy and a market-oriented economy. A more robust civil society could now begin to emerge. For an indefinite period, however, there could be considerable political turmoil of the kind that befell post-1990 Nicaragua. Cuba's fragile democracy would remain threatened by *fidelista-raulista* control of the Army and by the Communist Party's ability to order strikes and antigovernment demonstrations.

This assessment suggests that some policies may lead to better outcomes than others, although even the better ones appear less than ideal. Furthermore, there are both limits and uncertainties about whether even the "best" policy can produce the positive outcome expected of it. As was noted in *Storm Warnings for Cuba*, Castro, his regime, and the Cuban populace appear to march to their own drum. Nevertheless, there still may be ways for the United States and its allies to oblige Cuba to pick up the pace of change over the next year or two.

Chapter Eight

A PROACTIVE POLICY FOR CUBA

It may not be possible to achieve a soft landing in Cuba. The regime's intransigence and the weakness of civil society and opposition groups may make peaceful change from above or below unlikely. If so, Cuba would be headed toward an uncontrolled-crisis situation in which stasis and heightened state repression occur under one endgame, or growing civil strife, military defections, and possible civil war ensue under another endgame (see the Appendix).

This concluding chapter will not propose a policy for dealing with a Cuba in an uncontrolled crisis. In 1994, *Storm Warnings for Cuba* outlined specific diplomatic, political, and military measures for coping with a Cuba spinning out of control. Those recommendations hold for 1996 and beyond.[1]

Instead, the analysis in this chapter assumes that Cuba remains under the control of the Castro regime and that the regime continues to resist fundamental reforms under market-Leninism. As of December 1995, this appears to be the island's most likely future in the years immediately ahead.

Although current U.S. policy looks better than the prevailing alternatives, policymakers may wish to consider a bolder, proactive strategy that would seek to outflank the Cuban dictator. While maintaining

---

[1]The study recommended that U.S. policy proceed simultaneously along two tracks: On Track One, U.S. policy would deal with a Cuba that remained in a controlled-crisis situation. On Track Two, the United States would prepare itself for an uncontrolled crisis on the island through measures aimed at containing, alleviating, and resolving the crisis. See Gonzalez and Ronfeldt, *Storm Warnings for Cuba*, 1994, pp. 138–150.

the embargo, or at least its ban on U.S. investments and credits and on aid and loans to Cuba from international agencies, this strategy would target Cuba's agents of change to hasten the island's peaceful or less-violent transition toward a democratic, market-oriented system.[2]

AGENTS OF CHANGE AND THEIR PARALYSIS

There are actors within Cuban society who yearn for fundamental change. Among them are students, intellectuals, artists, workers, and would-be entrepreneurs, as well as more-outspoken dissidents, human-rights activists, and those in opposition circles. These are the agents of change outside the regime that the U.S. policy could help bolster if Track II of the CDA were expanded and fully implemented.

There are also agents of change within the regime who are not adequately addressed by current policy. They include the *reformistas*, who are attempting to promote change by working within the regime or in so-called NGOs that remain closely connected to the government. They occupy mid- and upper-level posts in the government bureaucracy, the Party, and the military, or they work in research centers, universities, and other government-affiliated institutions.

Were they to work together, these potential agents of change might be able to effect peaceful change from above and below. With but a few exceptions, however, many remain politically inert for any number of reasons: They fear the state's pervasive security apparatus, the prospects of social upheaval, the return of vengeful right-wing exiles, and/or the unknown consequences of a Cuba without Castro. Some expect that at a propitious time they can leave Cuba, legally or illegally. Others, especially those associated with the regime, may still cling to the hope that Castro himself will finally embrace change or that Raúl will be able to push through needed reforms. Still others are simply resigned to there being no change in the foreseeable future.

---

[2]"Proactive" has become a code word used by liberal and leftist writers who want Washington to lift the embargo in the expectation that doing so will encourage the Castro regime's evolution toward a less authoritarian form of socialism. The strategy outlined in the following pages is quite different in its assumptions, instruments, and aims.

This political inertia produces a strong asymmetry in motivation between those who would like to see change but are too risk-averse to take action, and those who are determined to hold onto power and to preserve the regime by whatever means necessary. As a consequence, the former have refrained from actively pushing for deeper reforms, whether from below or from above.

Although immobilized at present, these agents of change constitute the basis for a broad coalition, formal or informal, that could work to accelerate Cuba's transition to a democratic, market-oriented society. Conceivably, they might become the future nucleus of a post-Castro government. In the meantime, they need the right circumstances and incentives to act and coalesce in a mutually reinforcing fashion that would strengthen their respective roles inside and outside the regime so that fundamental change in Cuba can occur.

Eastern Europe is instructive in this respect. Cuba is not likely to follow Poland's path because of the weakness of the island's civil society. It is hoped that Cuba will not be another Romania, where an internal regime coup against the Ceausescu dictatorship led to considerable bloodletting and not much system change. However, Cuba might end by resembling East Germany in 1989.

In East Germany, Lutheran pastors, reform-minded communist leaders, and members of the intelligentsia, including some who had collaborated with the regime and the secret police, came together in an informal coalition. They provided the political leadership and moral authority that led to mass demonstrations in Leipzig against the communist government and the defection of the army. The United States may be able to induce Cuba to move forward along the lines of the East German example.

ORCHESTRATING THE CATALYST FOR CHANGE

Building on, but moving beyond, Track II of the Cuban Democracy Act, the United States should reach out to Cuba's agents of change to accelerate the island's transition to a more liberalized polity and economy. Ideally, such a transition would take place peacefully under a broad-based coalition government of national reconciliation that would include civilian and military reformers from the current regime, along with dissidents, opposition leaders, and representatives of Cuba's civil society. This would be a desirable Cuban endgame. However, in the final analysis, it is an outcome that hinges on Cuba's own political dynamics.

Targeting Regime Reformers

If U.S. policy is to serve as a catalytic agent for peaceful system change, then it should first target the regime's civilian and military reformers, because they are in a strategic position to initiate fundamental political and economic transformations—with or without Castro. Indeed, the underlying message that needs to be communicated to these elites through public diplomacy is that their future is not irrevocably tied to the continued presence of either Fidel or Raúl.

The new policy initiatives, consequently, need to go beyond the democratic and market-oriented goals stipulated by the Cuban Democracy Act. They must go beyond the promise in the Helms-Burton bill to lift the embargo and extend economic, technical, and military assistance to a democratic Cuba. Rather, employing public diplomacy by means of Radio Martí, press conferences, and other public forums, U.S. officials need to clarify U.S. intentions toward a Cuba in transition. In contrast to Helms-Burton, they need to send unambiguous signals toward those regime actors who actively promote Cuba's liberalization and who would thus be eligible to participate in a new government of national reconciliation.

The new policy initiatives should seek to deepen the existing or potential fissures in the Castro regime. To do so, they should employ inducements to embolden the regime's reformist elements, as well as the political opposition on the outside, to work actively for a new Cuba. The goal would be to bring about fundamental system change through internal forces—the agents of change—acting from above and from below.

To reassure regime reformists, for example, the President, Secretaries of State and Defense, and other high U.S. officials should reiterate publicly that the United States will

- refrain from undertaking armed aggression against a Cuba that is undergoing change

- prevent extremist exile groups from conducting raids that could precipitate a wider conflict with the Cuban armed forces

- respect the sovereignty and independence of a new Cuba

- encourage Cuban-Americans, other U.S. businesses, and international financial institutions to invest in and extend loans and credit to a new Cuba

- acknowledge the central role that current civilian and military reformers could play in a post-Castro Cuba, including in a government of national reconciliation.

The Revolutionary Armed Forces are clearly the most important institution to be targeted under a proactive policy. The military will be the key player in determining whether the current transition process leads to a more democratic, market-oriented Cuba. The FAR will, in any event, emerge as the strongest institution in a post-Castro Cuba. Although now loyal to the Castro brothers, individual officers may become less supportive if the island's economic and political conditions deteriorate further, if officers conclude that the regime cannot resolve the crisis, if they see that the regime's policies are damaging the military's institutional interests, and, most important, if they are offered a way out of Cuba's dilemma.

Thus, the United States needs to begin reaching out to the Cuban military. As a start, the Department of State should lift the long-standing ban on U.S. military attachés having contact with their Cuban counterparts in third countries. Confidence-building measures should also be undertaken by the Department of Defense, such as inviting FAR representatives to U.S. military exercises in the Caribbean. To be sure, Raúl and the MINFAR will order Cuban officers to rebuff, ignore, and report on U.S. overtures. But if this happens, then FAR officers will know that it is Havana, rather than Washington, that is preventing professional contact between the two military establishments.

If the above steps are to help provide a catalyst for effecting peaceful change on the island, the administration will need to carefully craft and orchestrate its initiatives toward Cuba. It will also have to convince key sectors of the Cuban-American community that, given present realities in Cuba, these efforts to target the regime's civilian and military reformers offer the best chance for a peaceful transition in Cuba. The cost, which admittedly will be high for the more conservative exile circles, will be that some members of the Castro regime will play a role in a coalition government of national reconciliation.

Targeting Civil Society Actors

If dissidents, opposition leaders, and other representatives from civil society are ultimately to participate in a government of national reconciliation, then U.S. policy also needs to redouble efforts to strengthen civil society actors in Cuba. Some measures are already stipulated under Track II of the Cuban Democracy Act, but others should be taken:

- Increase information flows to and from the island and within the island, and continue the promotion of electronic communications, including via fax machines, computers, software, and e-mail linkages.

- Decentralize and expand communication networks on the island, for example, by allowing U.S. manufacturers to market cellular phones in Cuba.

- Increase contacts and exchanges with Cuban intellectuals, dissidents, and human-rights activists, even if Havana denies visas to some Americans.

- Encourage European and U.S. NGOs to strengthen ties with Cuba's nascent independent labor movement, human-rights organizations, and other fledgling NGOs.

- Aid individuals and NGOs in becoming more financially independent of the Cuban state, for example, by rescinding the ban on cash remittances.

In addition to preparing them for future power-sharing, the strengthening of civil society actors would help speed the transition to a new Cuba. Currently deprived of access to organized popular support, the regime's reformers feel too isolated and vulnerable to push hard for systemic changes. But a more robust civil society could strengthen the reformers' hand as they maneuver to bring about change from above, because they would find supportive allies outside the regime. Cuba's transition process would thus be propelled by the combined forces of change from above and from below.[3]

Hastening Change by Means of the "Grand Bargain"

In attempting to outflank Castro, it is possible that U.S. policy will oblige the Cuban leader to undertake major reforms to remain at the helm and in command of his government. But doing so would be out of character for the *lider máximo*. In 37 years of ruling Cuba, he has neither been a democrat nor a free-marketeer. He has been and remains a socialist *caudillo* who adamantly opposes any form of liberalization that would erode his power and undermine cherished socialist and revolutionary principles.

The more likely scenario, therefore, is that Castro will continue to block, slow, and emasculate liberalizing reforms proposed by some of his subordinates. If so, Cuba will require the departure of its "great helmsman" to avert a social explosion and clear the way for change, in the same fashion that Mao Zedong's death in 1976 made possible China's subsequent economic transformation. Hence, the United States should pursue an approach that encourages civilian and military reformers to move against the Cuban leader and his hardline followers.

Toward this end, the U.S. Government could publicly offer Castro *and* Cuba something like the grand bargain that was first proposed in *Storm Warnings for Cuba*. The "grand bargain" was a gambit originally intended to leave Castro's dignity intact and elevate his image as a statesman by encouraging his resignation from office in order to

---

[3]Many of the above policy initiatives toward regime elites and civil society actors are similar to the policy prescriptions issued by the Inter-American Dialogue. There are two major differences, however. First, contrary to the Dialogue's recommendation, this author is opposed to Cuba being admitted to the International Monetary Fund and the World Bank until there is a deeper, irreversible commitment by the Castro regime to genuine market reforms for the *entire* Cuban economy. Second, whereas the Dialogue seeks to encourage a step-by-step accommodation by both the U.S. and Cuban governments on the basis of specific concessions by each, the aim of this author's strategy is to help produce those conditions within Cuba that will compel the present government, with or without Castro, to embark upon fundamental systemic change as a requisite for normalizing relations. See Inter-American Dialogue, *Cuba in the Americas*, 1995, pp. 3–8.

head off civil war on the island.[4] In this instance, however, Washington would propose the grand bargain before an uncontrolled crisis developed. Its purpose would be to provide a clear signal to Cuban leaders, dissidents, and others in the population that the U.S. Government was committed to helping them achieve peaceful change on the island with or without Castro.

In this version of the grand bargain, the United States would publicly propose that Castro relinquish his power to a provisional coalition government that would be recognized by the United States. Once the Cuban leader (and presumably many of his followers) left the island, the embargo would be lifted, and normal travel and economic ties would be fully restored. Internationally supervised elections for a new constitution and government would follow. In exchange, the United States would commit itself to turning over the U.S. Naval Base at Guantánamo to the newly elected Cuban Government, respecting Cuba's sovereignty and independence, and helping Cuba secure needed international credit, markets, and investments.

Of course, the Castro brothers and their followers would reject and ridicule the U.S. proposal. But their doing so is of little consequence. The purpose of the grand bargain is to help set in motion new political dynamics among key civilian and military circles, and sectors of the population at large, that will encourage them to act on behalf of fundamental change in Cuba. Were the United States to propose to them something along the lines of the grand bargain, these actors may conclude that Castro has ceased to be indispensable, that they now have a way out of Cuba's political and economic predicament, and that the *comandante* and his like-minded cohorts must go.

THE LIMITATIONS OF A PROACTIVE POLICY

Castro recognizes that a U.S. policy that targets both regime reformers and civil society actors poses a threat to his regime. In his July 26, 1995, speech, the Cuban leader attacked Track II of the Cuban

---

[4]Gonzalez and Ronfeldt proposed the "grand bargain" under Track Two of their two-track strategy for a United States dealing with Cuba in crisis. The grand bargain is a way of ending Cuba's uncontrolled crisis, heading off U.S. intervention, and securing Castro's resignation. See Gonzalez and Ronfeldt, *Storm Warnings for Cuba*, 1994, pp. 143–147.

Democracy Act almost as much as the embargo's proposed tightening under the Helms-Burton bill. Whereas extremist exile circles and Helms-Burton sought to strangle Cuba outright, according to Castro, the designers of Track II want

> to infiltrate us, weaken us, to create all types of counterrevolutionary organizations, and to destabilize the country regardless of the consequences. . . . These people want to exert their influence through broad exchanges with diverse sectors that they consider vulnerable, to grant doubtful scholarships, and to dazzle us with billion-dollar institutions, their technology, and their social research centers.

He went on to complain bitterly that Track II aims "to destroy us from within."[5]

Raúl Castro echoed his brother the following November in a speech commemorating the founding of Military Counterintelligence. He denounced Track II as a "rotten carrot" that sought to subvert the Cuban regime's "fighting spirit and awareness."[6] Thus, the Castro leadership can be expected to react even more vigorously to a proactive policy that goes beyond the provisions and intent of Track II of the CDA to target the regime's military and civilian elites.

From the U.S. perspective, a proactive policy of the kind outlined above does have its intrinsic limitations. The following three may render it a difficult policy to manage and sustain over any length of time.

First, the policy is not likely to work unless economic conditions deteriorate or do not improve in Cuba over the course of the next year or two. If the economy continues to improve, foreign investments flow in, and social tensions ease, then the agents of change, both inside and outside the regime, are likely to resign themselves to the status quo—as appears to be the case at present. Only when conditions deteriorate further, stasis sets in, and Cuba's future again appears bleak can we expect such agents to risk their positions and possibly their lives in an attempt to hasten the pace of change. This limitation

---

[5]"Fidel Castro Speaks," 1995, pp. 7, 8.

[6]"Raúl Castro Discusses," 1995, p. 8.

would thus argue for keeping the embargo in place, but without implementing the politically threatening, counterproductive measures contained in Helms-Burton.

Second, even if conditions were to deteriorate, a proactive policy is a long-term strategy for promoting change. Because it must depend on actors in Cuba becoming sufficiently emboldened to act, the policy is not likely to yield results quickly. Thus, the policy may be difficult to sustain over time, given the partisan nature of U.S. politics and the pressures of the more militant anti-Castro sectors of the Cuban-American community. Indeed, right-wing exiles are likely to denounce the policy because of its overtures toward leadership circles within the current regime.

Third, to work, the proposed proactive policy will require a high degree of policy consensus, direction, and coordination that may well be beyond the capacity of the politically and bureaucratically divided U.S. Government. The policy will need to find support not only in Congress but also throughout the Executive Branch. It will need constant attention and fine-tuning by high-level policymakers. Ironically, a proactive policy may be less suited to Washington than to the highly centralized, personalistic decisionmaking system that exists in Castro's Cuba.

Yet, with all its limitations, the proactive policy may be able to attract broader public support than can either the present policy or its existing alternatives, because it rests on principles that appeal to conservatives, moderates, and liberals. The proactive policy aims at promoting peaceful change toward a democratic, market-oriented Cuba by appealing to internal actors on the island, including those inside as well as outside the regime. It promises not only a Cuba after Castro that is free, independent, and sovereign, but also one that retains many of the social gains achieved under the Cuban Revolution.

In this respect, the proposed strategy would build on the existing policy consensus already contained in the Helms-Burton bill with regard to the composition of a future government in a post-Castro Cuba. As was noted in Chapter Seven, both the House and Senate versions of Helms-Burton pledge that the U.S. Government will be impartial toward any individual or organization elected by the Cuban people, except that the new government cannot include the Castro brothers and the regime's present security organs must be dissolved. Consequently, most current leadership circles, whether civilian or military, reformist or centrist, need not fear U.S. reprisals against them, even under Helms-Burton. The proactive policy would go a step further by actively targeting these leadership actors through public diplomacy and confidence-building measures.

On balance, therefore, conservatives, moderates, and liberals may be able to support the proactive policy because it resonates with many—although by no means all—of their respective values and policy aims. And by assuming a bolder, less ambiguous stance and tying together elements of existing or proposed policy, the proactive alternative makes for a more coherent strategy for promoting peaceful change in Cuba.

Since this study's completion in early December 1995, Cuban developments have taken a turn for the worse. In mid-December, Castro signaled that he was again applying the brakes to economic reforms by dismissing his Minister of Investments and Cooperation, Ernesto Melendez Bach, a *reformista*. A new crackdown on the internal opposition followed in February 1996, when state security agents arrested some 100 members of *Concilio Cubano*, thereby crushing *Concilio's* plans for civil disobedience. Then, on February 24, after having engaged in earlier violations of Cuban airspace and the dropping of leaflets, two unarmed Cessnas flown by the Cuban-American humanitarian group Brothers to the Rescue were destroyed by Cuban MiGs.

According to Castro, the February 24 action had been agreed upon weeks earlier by him, his brother, and the Joint Chiefs of Staff, because they were fed up with the flagrant air intrusions by Brothers to the Rescue and "people were criticizing the Cuban air force."[1] However, he may well have had additional political ends in mind when he approved an action that was certain to provoke a firestorm of criticism in the United States, cost his government much international goodwill, and discourage new Western investments in Cuba.

Following as it did on the heels of rising internal repression at home, the shooting down of the two Cessnas served Castro's political purposes by demonstrating that his regime would use whatever force it deemed necessary to quash its opponents. Through the air force's

---

[1]See Kathy Booth, "Interview: Fidel's Defense," *Time*, March 11, 1996, p. 38.

commission of an atrocity, the Cuban dictator also compromised the FAR and showed that the military would fire on civilians in defense of his regime. In turn, the air incident now makes future contacts between the U.S. military and Cuban military—something that he and his brother had become uneasy about—more difficult than ever. And by heightening tension with the Cuban exile community and the United States, he created a new siege atmosphere with which to rally supporters in and outside his regime.

The February 24 incident has had a dramatic effect on U.S. policy toward Cuba, severely undermining the position of those critics who had been calling for the lifting of the embargo. Following the incident, President Clinton ordered the suspension of all charter flights to Cuba, the imposition of wider sanctions against Havana, and the convening of the UN Security Council, which unanimously deplored the Cuban action. Most telling, the White House negotiated an agreement with Congress on the stalled Helms-Burton bill, which the Senate and House of Representatives overwhelmingly passed in early March and which President Clinton is expected to sign.

Henceforth, under the somewhat-altered Helms-Burton Act, the embargo will be tightened so stringently that foreign companies doing business in Cuba could face lawsuits in U.S. courts. Equally important, the embargo has been locked into U.S. law, to be lifted or eased only by Congress. A new, tougher U.S. stance toward Havana will thus complement the stasis that Castro's Cuba is virtually certain to undergo during the remainder of 1996 and beyond.

ACTORS, MODELS, AND ENDGAMES

In *Storm Warnings for Cuba*, which was completed in June 1994, the authors developed five endgames—essentially, future outcomes—that they believed could materialize for a Cuba in transition. With modifications as well as updating, I have now selected four of these endgames for projecting Cuba's most likely futures over the next one to three years while holding current U.S. policy constant.[1] In each, I identify the role of key regime and nonregime actors and highlight the policy implications for the United States.

All four endgames start from two premises. First, current U.S. policy remains in force: The embargo is neither tightened further nor lifted. Second, the regime continues to move toward a "market-Leninist" model in which there is partial, state-directed economic liberalization combined with authoritarian rule. The endgames are divided into two sets:

- In the first set, Cuba remains in a *controlled-crisis* situation, in which the regime muddles through and survives (Endgame I).

- In the second set, Cuba enters into an *uncontrolled-crisis* situation, in which there is stasis and increased state repression (Endgame II), a transition to a coalition government (Endgame III), or violent system change in the wake of military defections and civil unrest (Endgame IV).

---

[1]See Gonzalez and Ronfeldt, *Storm Warnings for Cuba* (pp. 71–116). The first endgame—"crisis and transition to another model"—has been omitted from this study because Cuba now appears to have moved beyond that stage.

No linear progression is imputed to the endgames discussed below. Cuba may, in fact, oscillate between different endgames in the months and years ahead.

ENDGAME I: THE REGIME MUDDLES THROUGH

Basic Scenario

Cuba remains in a controlled-crisis situation in which the regime's control apparatus, more than its economic policies, continues to account for the Castro government's survival. The regime is able to impose its will on society and governs without encountering serious organized opposition. The state remains strong, and its controls are pervasive. Civil society remains too weak to assert its independence effectively, much less to challenge the state—in contrast, for example, to Poland in the 1980s. The regime retains its relative cohesiveness, because most Party cadres, security personnel, and military officers have a strong personal stake in the regime's survival. They see alternatives to Castro as not being viable and as threatening to their power, status, and privileges.

Slow Economic Recovery, Continued Stability

The Cuban economy has yet to recover to the level of activity it achieved in the 1980s. Consumer goods, petroleum, and other basic necessities remain in short supply. Life continues to be hard for the vast majority of Cubans, especially those earning fixed salaries and wages. Particularly hard hit are workers who have been laid off from jobs in state enterprises and cannot find employment; their monthly unemployment payments amount to 60 percent of their former wages at a time when inflation continues to boost the price of goods and services.

Nevertheless, the economic free fall that characterized the 1991–1994 period has slowed significantly. Modest increases in foreign investments and tourism and in foreign-exchange earnings from sugar and nickel exports have gradually begun to improve the island's economic outlook. The enactment of additional, albeit still-modest, liberalizing measures for the domestic economy, especially the expansion of private-sector activity, has helped to hold down unemployment as well as to ease economic austerity.

However, political considerations continue to dictate economic policy. Far more so than in China or Vietnam, the regime continues to guard against the emergence of an independent Cuban bourgeoisie by strictly limiting the size, domain, and profitability of Cuban-owned firms. As in recent years, it prefers to establish state-chartered joint enterprises in such foreign-exchange-producing activities as tourism and biotechnology, and to have these firms run by loyalists drawn from the government, Party, and military. It also continues to favor collective or cooperative ownership of farms over private ownership.

Endgame Implications

This endgame essentially consolidates current conditions in Cuba. It would not do much to disturb the present distribution of power: The state would remain overwhelmingly strong; most civil society actors, with the exception of the Catholic Church, would continue to be weak. Within the regime, power and authority relationships would also remain pretty much as in today's Cuba. Hence, the *centristas* under Raúl Castro would remain the dominant policy tendency, sometimes supported by the *duros*, sometimes by the *reformistas*, depending on the policy in question. Although the Communist Party retains its vanguard status on political issues in particular, more and more economic administration and control shifts to the Army as an institution, and to active-duty or retired officers who direct tourist firms and support facilities, joint enterprises backed by foreign capital, military industrial enterprises, and agricultural complexes. Similarly, the Yummies continue to find new opportunities in the state and external sectors of the economy.

How would this endgame affect the United States? In some respects, a politically stable, economically viable Cuba would be less disruptive to the rest of the Caribbean and would perhaps pose fewer problems to U.S. interests. A stable, cohesive government would be better able to maintain law and order on the island and to comply with Cuba's international commitments. This, together with an economy that no longer is in free fall, suggests that uncontrolled out-migration from the island to the United States and other Caribbean

Basin countries could be kept in check. Also, a government that has effective power and authority might make the island less open to drug-trafficking by the Colombian and other drug cartels—provided, of course, that the regime is committed to enforcing an antidrug policy.

On the other hand, the continued survival of the Castro regime in essentially its present form and composition could present problems for the United States. Cuba would continue to be dominated by the Castro brothers, by their hardline and centrist followers, and by the Party, the military, and the security organs—not by genuine reformers who advocate system change toward a market economy and a more open polity. All share a strong anti–U.S. animus and authoritarian values. While Castro has been the most visceral and extreme in his attacks on "imperialism," his stance probably reflects the sentiments of many of his hardline and centrist followers, as does his open contempt for Western democracy.

Thus, at a time when the postcommunist world has witnessed the reemergence of democratic forces in Latin America and a new harmony in inter-American relations, Castro's authoritarian regime would remain entrenched on the island. It would remain a source of antidemocratic sentiment and inter-American friction in the Caribbean and Latin America. It could provide refuge for revolutionary activists and other antidemocratic forces. In December 1994, for example, Castro personally welcomed Lt. Colonel Hugo Chávez to Havana and commended him for his attempted military coup against Venezuela's democratically elected government.

For political as well as economic reasons, the Castro government could also allow Cuba to be used as a staging base for drug-traffickers, as it did prior to the Ochoa trial in 1989. Drug money would provide a quick fix for an economy that was stalled or not improving. The regime could rationalize Cuba's participation in drug-trafficking as a reprisal against U.S. hostility and economic sanctions. Even if not sanctioned by the regime, the money to be made in facilitating drug shipments through Cuban airspace and territorial waters would be certain to attract corruptible, financially strapped government officials, particularly in the Ministry of Interior and the armed forces.

In the long run, the survival of the Castro regime would probably worsen Cuba's economic plight rather than resolve it, given the resistance of the dominant leadership circles to more-sweeping reforms. Thus, even if Cuba became more like a Caribbean Vietnam, migration pressures among the island's population could remain high in the years ahead if economic conditions failed to improve markedly. For the same reason, anti-regime sentiment among the populace most likely would continue to grow.

Such a Cuba is not likely to trigger a change in U.S. policy. Unless the Castro regime were to change course and liberalize its policies, Washington would find it difficult to engage in a policy of "calibrated response," because of the absence of fundamental political and economic reforms. Lifting the embargo would be even more difficult under such conditions.

As a consequence, Cuba would remain politically volatile. As is currently the situation, stability would depend on the regime's ability to maintain a tight lid on the populace through the presence of its coercive organs of state power and on the populace's remaining relatively passive. Yet, the possibility would always exist that an unanticipated spark—an incident involving the police, repeated power failures during hot weather, renewed consumer-goods shortages, unexpected crop failures, etc.—could cause a popular explosion to erupt in Havana or other cities.

ENDGAME II: HEIGHTENED AUTHORITARIANISM AND STASIS

In this endgame, economic and political conditions worsen; Cuba is plunged into an uncontrolled-crisis situation. Much of the island, especially Havana, experiences mounting political unrest and violence of a greater magnitude than occurred with the riots in August 1994. Unlike in that situation, the regime's security organs—Ministry of Interior Special Troops, Rapid Reaction Brigades, and the police— are unable to contain the rioting by students and unemployed or employed workers. Loyal Army units are called in by Castro; they restore order and regain control of the streets through the deployment of massive force. Meanwhile, Castro and the hardliners halt further reforms and rule through heavy-handed repression. Heightened authoritarianism and stasis in the reform process are the order of the day. Confronted with a hostile population, the regime hunkers down.

A Post-Tiananmen-Square-Like Situation

This endgame resembles the China of 1989 during and after the Tiananmen Square crackdown. It is marked by the marginalization of the reformers and the renewed dominance of hardliners within the regime. The centrists remain in charge of economic affairs, because of their close association with Raúl and their needed financial and managerial skills. Even so, the current political situation works against them; for the time being, they are unable to initiate any more-modest liberalizing measures.

A major shift in the relative power and influence of institutional players also takes place within the regime. The Party has been weakened because of its inability to govern and control the crisis. The Ministry of Interior (MININT) loses influence as well because it has failed to anticipate and contain the unrest. In contrast, the power and influence of the Revolutionary Armed Forces increase significantly because of the Army's pivotal role in preventing the downfall of the regime in the face of a budding popular insurrection. While this redounds to Raúl Castro's advantage by virtue of his rank as General of the Army and his position as Minister of the Revolutionary Armed Forces, it also means that, more than ever, the regime has become critically dependent on the continued loyalty and support of the FAR's generals and senior officers. Meanwhile, to ensure a more compliant society, the MINFAR assumes tighter control over the civilian-based Territorial Troop Militia and conscripts more young men into the Youth Labor Army.[2]

The military's preeminence leads to new emphasis being placed on strengthening and improving the performance of the state sector of the economy. Unlike the *reformistas*, the FAR is not particularly keen

---

[2]Over 1 million strong, the Territorial Troop Militia (MTT) is commanded by Division General Raúl Menendez Tommassevich, a *raulista* who fought with Raúl Castro during the guerrilla struggle. The Party also plays a political role in the MTT. Employed in agriculture and other activities in the countryside, the Youth Labor Army has long been an appendage of the FAR.

on further opening the domestic economy to the market and private enterprise. The corporate and personal interests of military officers lie in taking over the administration of inefficiently run state enterprises and introducing market mechanisms and Western managerial techniques to make those operations more productive and cost-effective. Their interests also lie in the state's establishing additional joint enterprises with foreign capital that, on the Cuban side, are under the management of active-duty and retired officers.

Endgame Implications

Even more so than the first, this endgame augurs poorly for Cuba and the United States. With the FAR institutionally dominant and hardliners in control, Cuban society could become increasingly militarized, and political dissent could be even more heavily repressed. Spanish, British, Canadian, and other foreign investments, along with tourism, would surely dry up because of concern over renewed popular unrest and heightened repression. These adverse developments, together with falling production levels resulting from workers' alienation, would be certain to accelerate the island's economic decline.

In turn, migration pressures would greatly intensify as more and more Cubans tried to escape the island's oppressive conditions, sometimes with the connivance of the government, as occurred in August and September 1994. While most of the out-migration would probably be attempted through the Florida Straits or the Guantánamo Naval Base, neighboring Caribbean islands are also certain to become destination points for the fleeing Cubans. In addition, this endgame could well result in the regime turning the island into a major transshipment point for illegal drugs, as a means of obtaining desperately needed cash and arms.

This endgame would result in increasing tension between Cuba and the United States and Cuba and other Caribbean nations. The Cuban-American community and other U.S. circles would demand that strong action be taken against Cuba's worsening dictatorship. Democratic governments in the Caribbean Basin would also deplore conditions in Cuba. For their part, Castro, the hardliners, and the military might try to exploit and exacerbate tensions with the United States and the exile community in Florida to create the external threat perception needed to maintain the FAR's cohesion and loyalty, and to mobilize the civilian populace in support of the regime.

For instance, incidents in the Florida Straits or on the Guantánamo Naval Base, whether involving exile attacks or islanders trying to reach freedom, could be used to put the FAR and Cuba on a war footing. Cuba would thus become a hostile garrison state, increasingly isolated from, and in tension with, many of its neighbors in the Caribbean. Such conditions would make it virtually impossible for Washington to consider a more flexible policy toward Cuba.

Because it represents stasis and increased repression, this endgame would become inherently unstable. The worsening state of the economy—caused by the stoppage of reforms, foreign investments, and tourism, and by the reliance on open, heavy-handed coercion—would accelerate regime delegitimation in the eyes of the civilian populace. Such delegitimation might also occur within the ranks of the FAR itself, because the regime's policies would now be eroding the prestige and image of the military as a national institution. Externally, too, the regime would find itself becoming isolated and with fewer friends in the hemisphere, including among the Latin American left. This endgame may thus set the stage for other endgames that also involve uncontrolled-crisis situations.

ENDGAME III: NONVIOLENT CHANGE AND POWER-SHARING

This endgame entails a power-sharing arrangement between civilian and military reformers in the Castro regime, and elements of the anti-Castro opposition in and outside Cuba. It results from a combination of pressures for change from below among the general population, and from above among civilian and military elites within the regime itself.

Change from Above and Below

The economy's sharp deterioration produces growing anti-regime opposition among the populace at large. In contrast to the previous endgame, however, this mass opposition becomes more organized and widespread. Divisions within the regime sharpen as civilian reformers split with the hardliners, centrists, and Castro brothers. They find allies among younger, progressive military officers who also want fundamental system change. Both forge links with opposition groups outside the regime who increasingly rally around the Catholic Church, which is seen as the only independent institution in Cuba.

At some point in this endgame, whether through accident, assassination, natural death, or forced resignation, Fidel Castro is no longer around, leaving a momentary leadership vacuum. With the support of Army units under the command of progressive officers, and that of the populace at large, reformist leaders seize power and a new coalition government is formed. The new government encounters resistance from hardline civilian and military leaders and from the Special Troops of the Ministry of Interior but is able to defeat the loyalists with minimal fighting.

Once in power, the new coalition government rapidly begins to enact liberalizing economic reforms. To help ease the effects of a rapid transition to a market economy, it tries to preserve some of the Castro government's social safety net. The new government commits itself to democracy and pledges free elections once the political situation has stabilized. For all practical purposes, nonviolent change has begun to be implemented in a post-Castro Cuba.

As emphasized in *Storm Warnings for Cuba*, Castro's departure is *the* requisite condition for this endgame to occur, because he is adamantly opposed to sharing power with anyone, let alone elements of the opposition. Thus, as long as Castro is present, this endgame remains unlikely. On the other hand, his absence from the scene would immediately increase its chances of materializing.

However, other conditions would have to be met for this endgame to take place. The populace would have to break out of its passivity and engage in direct acts of defiance against the regime. This change could provide the regime's reformist circles with the potential for mass support and, together with the growing specter of civil war, embolden them to turn against the regime. Most critically in this regard, reformist officers within the FAR, particularly key units of the Central and Western Armies, would have to defect from the regime, move against Raúl Castro, and support the new coalition.

Therefore, this scenario depends on the perception by military officers that their personal interests, and the interests of the FAR as an institution, are jeopardized as a result of the country's deterioration and the regime's ill-conceived policies. If there is fear that the uncontrolled crisis could end with the Army being ordered to fire on civilians, some of the FAR's most senior and respected generals might join the new coalition to spare the nation from further turmoil and salvage their personal honor.

Endgame Implications

This endgame would be best for the United States and the Caribbean. It would see the replacement of the Castro regime by a new government that would be market- and democratically oriented, and committed to national reconciliation and cooperation with Cuba's neighbors, including the United States. Such a government could reach out to moderate and nonviolent sectors of the Cuban exile community and would welcome U.S. and other Western capital investments to promote Cuba's speedy economic recovery. If stability prevailed on the island and the economy showed signs of improvement as a result of the government's policies, the pressures for out-migration could be better controlled and managed to the benefit of the United States and Cuba's other neighbors. The new government would most likely commit itself to a strong drug-enforcement policy, if only to ensure the economic support of the United States and other lenders.

On the other hand, the obstacles facing such a coalition government and democracy cannot be minimized. Strong leadership would be required to keep the government and its disparate coalition together—without, however, a new *caudillo* arising. The government would have to try to govern democratically in the absence of a supportive civil society, and in a country lacking strongly rooted democratic traditions and institutions. Meanwhile, Cuba would be saddled with remnants of the 600,000-person-strong Communist Party, many of whose members would retain their authoritarian, vanguard mentality. The military and police would have to be purged of *fidelista* and *raulista* elements, to have democratic values instilled in them, and to be subordinated to new, untested civilian rule. In short, the transition to democratic rule would be a fragile, long, and not necessarily linear process in a post-Castro Cuba.

On balance, however, Endgame III still augurs the best future for both Cuba and the United States. Its real problem revolves around the preconditions that must be fulfilled before it can take place. In the absence of a U.S. policy that aggressively targets Cuba's agents of change, these preconditions are likely to render it an unlikely endgame.

ENDGAME IV: VIOLENT SYSTEM CHANGE

Basic Scenario

In this initially Romanian-like endgame, Castro and the hardliners continue to dominate the regime. Reforms are not enacted or, if they are, they are too little and too late to arrest the country's economic and political decline. Cuba is caught in an increasing cycle of mass protest and heavy-handed state repression. Castro seeks to hold onto the loyalty of the military and his rank-and-file civilian supporters by capitalizing on incidents with the United States, as when *balseros* seek to escape Cuban waters. But this tactic fails because the FAR starts to split into pro- and anti-regime camps.

Finally, a political explosion is triggered when mass protests erupt throughout the island and cannot be contained by the regime's security forces. Army units are now deployed; they refuse to fire on civilians, joining the protesting civilians instead. But other units remain loyal to the two Castro brothers, as do MININT's Special Troops. Cuba is plunged into civil war. As opposed to Endgame II, however, the civil conflict and Castro's growing international isolation lead to his regime's downfall and to radical system change.

In contrast to Endgame III, the polarization caused by *fidelista* rule and civil war lead neither to a coalition government nor to nonviolent change. Instead, a vengeful rightist government emerges and, together with its rank-and-file supporters, engages in repression and outright violence against those suspected of having supported the old regime. In this endgame, Cuba is reminiscent of post-1973 Chile following the downfall of the Allende government, but it lacks the civil society, democratic traditions, and institutions, including political parties, that helped mediate some of the severity of the Pinochet years.

With the exception of military officers who had turned against Castro, the new rightist government is composed of those who had not participated in the *fidelista* regime, and may have actively opposed it, whether on the island or from exile. The Communist Party is outlawed. Former security and government personnel and Party cadres are brought to trial and punished severely. Old scores against the old regime's rank-and-file followers and henchmen are settled at the grass-roots level. Although they constitute a majority of the population, Afro-Cubans and mulattos are discriminated against for having been the social beneficiaries and supporters of the *fidelista* revolution, thereby intensifying racial animosities stemming from the Castro era. Cuba is thus left ideologically, politically, and racially divided.

The new government's first priority is to spur Cuba's recovery through rapid conversion to a market economy. The government thus privatizes state and cooperative enterprises, welcomes Cuban exile and foreign capital, and encourages the development of private businesses. But the deals are often rigged to favor particular elites. Except for the elderly, the government provides little in the way of a social safety net to help out those left unemployed or without the financial resources or inclination to start their own businesses. At least initially, the new Cuba experiences large unemployment and a sort of "wild capitalism" similar to that found in Russia today.

The government also promises to hold democratic elections. But in contrast to Pinochet's Chile, there is no civil society or party system to pressure the government to restore democratic rule. Meanwhile, it must repair or create new institutions that can govern effectively in a Cuba that has suffered from decades of *fidelista* rule and recent civil strife.

Endgame Implications

While this endgame promises a future Cuba that resonates with the ideals of the free market and democracy, it presents some major problems for the United States and the Caribbean. In the civil-war phase of this endgame, the United States runs the risk of a military confrontation with the Castro regime (or its remnants), either because Castro engineers it or because of pressures from the Cuban-American community, Congress, and others to intervene to end the conflict and oust Castro. Military intervention in Cuba, however, would incur risks far greater than those encountered in Somalia or Haiti.

Even with a new post-Castro government in place, Cuba could become an open sore and a destabilizing factor in the Caribbean. More Cubans than ever—perhaps upwards of 2 or 3 million—would be forced by the political upheaval and economic wreckage caused by the civil war to try to emigrate from the island. Without strong government institutions, the island could become more open to drug-trafficking, especially if the post-Castro army and police lack professionalism. If civilian rule proves to be corrupt, ineffective, and turbulent, as it was under the 1944–1952 *Auténtico* administrations, Cuba could again witness the rise of another civilian or military dictator, further setting back democracy on the island.

CONCLUSIONS

Endgame III, in which a national coalition government succeeds the Castro regime, would provide the best post-Castro outcome for the United States and the Caribbean. However, it appears to be the least likely of all the endgames, unless U.S. policy succeeds in providing the catalyst for change. Endgame I, in which Cuba becomes a Caribbean Vietnam, may offer only short-term stability and a way station to an uncontrolled crisis situation over the longer term. To varying degrees, the remaining two endgames—stasis and repression, and violent change—bode badly for the United States and other Caribbean nations. Each carries with it high risks of military confrontation, and each could produce a polarized, economically shattered nation.

Abrams, Elliot, "Castro's Latest Coup," *National Review*, June 12, 1995, pp. 36–37.

Alfonso, Pablo, "Cita en La Habana de coalición disidente," *El Nuevo Herald* (Supplement to *The Miami Herald*), December 6, 1995, pp. 1A, 8A.

Amnesty International News Service, June 20, 1995.

Amnesty International Report 1995, "Cuba," as reprinted in Freedom House, *Cuba Brief*, June 1995.

"ANAP President Discusses Migration," *FBIS-LAT-95-216*, November 8, 1995, p. 4.

Atlantic Council of the United States, *A Road Map for Restructuring Future U.S. Relations with Cuba*, Washington, D.C., June 1995.

"Bank Overhaul Planned," *CubaNews*, December 1995, p. 2.

Booth, Kathy, "Interview: Fidel's Defense," *Time*, March 11, 1996, p. 38.

"BPIC Director Indamiro Restano Comments on Cuba, Castro," *FBIS-LAT-95-202*, October 19, 1995, p. 28.

Brzezinski, Zbigniew, "Facing Up to Consequences of a Castro Crash Landing," *Los Angeles Times*, September 7, 1994.

Business Monitor International, Ltd., *Latin American Monitor (Caribbean)*, November 1995, p. 6.

Castro, Max J., *Cuba: The Continuing Crisis*, Miami: University of Miami, The North-South Agenda, North-South Center, April 1995.

"Castro's Compromises," *Time*, February 20, 1995, p. 58.

CubaInfo, Vol. 6, No. 16, December 15, 1994.

"Cuba mantiene gastos reducidos de defensa," disseminated by Reuters News Service, *El Nuevo Herald*, November 30, 1994.

CubaNews, June 1995.

CubaNews, November 1995, p. 3.

"Cuba: Text of Foreign Investment Law," *FBIS-LAT-95-193-S*, October 5, 1995, pp. 1–11.

"Deputy Tourism Minister Notes Sector Development," *FBIS-LAT-95-202*, October 19, 1995, p. 27.

"Economic Growth," CubaNews, December 1995, p. 6.

"Experts Expect Better Harvest, Not Full Recovery," *CubaNews*, November 1995, p. 6.

FBIS-LAT-95-173-S, September 7, 1995, pp. 6, 8, 9.

"Fidel Castro Speaks at Moncada Ceremony," *FBIS-LAT-95-145*, July 28, 1995.

Golden, Tim, "A Year After Exodus, Threat to Castro Fades," *The New York Times*, August 15, 1995.

Gonzalez, Edward, and David Ronfeldt, *Castro, Cuba, and the World*, Santa Monica, Calif.: RAND, R-3420, June 1986.

———, *Cuba Adrift in a Postcommunist World*, Santa Monica, Calif.: RAND, R-4231-USDP, 1992.

———, *Storm Warnings for Cuba*, Santa Monica, Calif.: RAND, MR-452-OSD, June 1994.

Greenhouse, Steven, "To Undermine Castro, U.S. Plans Links with Cubans," *The New York Times*, June 12, 1995.

"Group Reports Arrest of Independent Journalist," *FBIS-LAT-95-207*, October 26, 1995, pp. 2–3.

Gunn, Gillian, *Cuba's NGOs: Government Puppets or Seeds of Civil Society?* Washington, D.C.: Georgetown University, Cuba Briefing Paper Series, No. 7, February 1995.

Hamilton, Lee H., and Claiborne Pell, "The Embargo Must Go," *The Washington Post,* September 8, 1994.

"The House Version: A Lot Tougher," *CubaNews,* November 1995, p. 7.

"Income Taxes Introduced," *CubaNews,* January 1996, p. 2.

Inter-American Dialogue, *Cuba in the Americas: Breaking the Policy Deadlock,* Washington, D.C.: The Second Report of the Inter-American Dialogue Task Force on Cuba, September 1995.

International Institute for Strategic Studies, *The Military Balance: 1995/1996,* London: Brassey's Inc., 1995.

International Republican Institute, *Dissenting Voices,* Vol. 1, No. 2, July 1995.

International Research 2000, Inc., *Military and Transition in Cuba,* March 17, 1995.

Johnson, Bryan T., and John P. Sweeney, "A Blueprint for a Free Cuba," *The Heritage Foundation Backgrounder,* March 23, 1995.

Karnow, Stanley, "Vietnam Now," *Smithsonian,* January 1996, pp. 32–42.

Klepak, Hal, "Cuban Security—Old Myths and New Realities," *Jane's Intelligence Review,* Vol. 7, No. 7, July 1995, pp. 334–335.

Knox, Paul, "Sherritt Breathes Life into Cuban Mine," *Globe and Mail,* July 31, 1995, p. B6.

López Oliva, Enrique, "Stirrings in Cuba: Religious Reawakening," *Christian Century,* October 1994.

Mesa-Lago, Carmelo, "Cuba's Economic Recovery—How Good Are Those 1995 Predictions?" *Cuba Brief,* Freedom House, June 1995.

Millett, Richard L., *Cuba's Armed Forces: From Triumph to Survival*, Washington, D.C.: Georgetown University, Cuba Briefing Paper Series, No. 4, September 1993.

Montes, A. B., *The Military Response to Cuba's Economic Crisis*, Washington, D.C.: Defense Intelligence Agency, August 1993.

"New Investment Law Debated: Would Widen Opportunities," *CubaNews*, August 1995.

"New Political Faces," *CubaNews*, August 1995.

Oden, Thomas C., "The Church Castro Couldn't Kill," *Christianity Today*, April 25, 1994.

"An Open Letter to the President of the United States: Castro's Days Are Numbered—Don't Bail Out a Failed Dictator!" A full-page advertisement by prominent Republicans and others, *The New York Times*, September 26, 1994.

Oppenheimer, Andres, *Castro's Final Hour—The Secret Story Behind the Coming Downfall of Communist Cuba*, New York: Simon and Schuster, 1992.

"Optimism Produces Economic Disclosure," *CubaNews*, December 1995, p. 6.

Payne, Douglas W., "Castro's Currency Racket," *Cuba Brief*, Freedom House, June 1995.

Pell, Claiborne, and Lee H. Hamilton, "The Embargo Must Go," *The Washington Post*, September 8, 1994.

Pérez-López, Jorge P., "Castro Tries Survival Strategy," *Transition—The Newsletter About Reforming Economies*, The World Bank, Vol. 6, No. 3, March 1995.

Radu, Michael, "Cuba's Transition: Institutional Lessons from Eastern Europe," *Journal of Interamerican Studies and World Affairs*, Vol. 37, No. 2, Summer 1995, pp. 83–111.

"Raúl Castro Discusses Talks with U.S.," *FBIS-LAT-95-223*, November 20, 1995, p. 8.

Renzoli, Jésus, personal interview, Washington, D.C., June 9, 1994.

Ritter, A.R.M., *Exploring Cuba's Alternative Economic Futures*, Ottawa, Canada: Carleton University, The Norman Paterson School of International Affairs, Development Studies Working Paper, No. 4, 1992.

Robbins, Carla Anne, "Civics Lessons—As Economy Struggles, Cubans Find a Crack in Castro's Control," *The Wall Street Journal*, June 19, 1995.

Rohter, Larry, "Critics Question Nicaraguan Army's Makeover," *The New York Times*, July 16, 1995.

——, "Cuba Gambles on Reversing Fall in Sugar Harvest," *The New York Times*, November 26, 1995, p. 3.

——, "Havana Moves to Ease the Way for Emigres Who Live in the U.S. to Invest in Cuba," *The New York Times*, November 7, 1995, p. A11.

——, "A Little Hope Pumps Up an Attitude," *The New York Times*, November 19, 1995, p. 3.

Roque Cabello, Marta Beatriz. "Nada que echar la javita," as disseminated by electronic mail on CubaNet, April 5, 1995.

"Russia, Cuba Sign Economic Pacts," *CubaNews*, November 5, 1995, p. 5.

"Senate Approves Weak Helms-Burton Law," *CubaNews*, November 1995, p. 7.

Shils, Edward, "The Virtue of Civil Society," *Government and Opposition*, Winter 1991.

"Smallest Sugar Crop Bodes Ill for Cuba," *The Miami Herald*, June 20, 1995, as disseminated by NVALDES%unmb.BITNET@pucc. PRINCETON.EDU.

"Sugar Harvest Committed," *CubaNews*, October 1995, p. 5.

"Tax Will Hit Elite Hardest," *CubaNews*, January 1996, p. 2.

"Trade Deals Signed with Moscow," *Latin American Monitor (Caribbean)*, Vol. 12, No. 11, November 1995, p. 5.

U.S. Congress, Senate, Select Committee on Intelligence, *Worldwide Intelligence Review, Hearing Before the Select Committee on Intelligence*, 104th Congress, 1st Session, 1995.

Valdes, Nelson P., "Cuban Political Culture: Between Betrayal and Death," in Sandor Halebsky and John M. Kirk, eds., *Cuba in Transition: Crisis and Transformation*, Boulder, Colo.: Westview Press, 1992, pp. 207–228.

Walker, Phyllis Greene, "Cuba's Revolutionary Armed Forces: Adapting in the New Environment," *Cuban Studies, Estudios Cubanos*, Vol. 96, forthcoming in January 1997.

"Why Change Is Needed," *CubaNews*, December 1995, p. 2.